Literary Criticism and Cultural Theory

William E. Cain, *General Editor*

For a full list of titles in this series, please visit www.routledge.com

Equity in English Renaissance Literature
Thomas More and Edmund Spenser
Andrew J. Majeske

"You Factory Folks Who Sing This Rhyme Will Surely Understand"
Culture, Ideology, and Action in the Gastonia Novels of Myra Page, Grace Lumpkin, and Olive Dargan
Wes Mantooth

"Visionary Dreariness"
Readings in Romanticism's Quotidian Sublime
Markus Poetzsch

Fighting the Flames
The Spectacular Performance of Fire at Coney Island
Lynn Kathleen Sally

Idioms of Self-Interest
Credit, Identity, and Property in English Renaissance Literature
Jill Phillips Ingram

Machine and Metaphor
The Ethics of Language in American Realism
Jennifer Carol Cook

"Keeping Up Her Geography"
Women's Writing and Geocultural Space in Twentieth-Century U.S. Literature and Culture
Tanya Ann Kennedy

Contested Masculinities
Crises in Colonial Male Identity from Joseph Conrad to Satyajit Ray
Nalin Jayasena

Unsettled Narratives
The Pacific Writings of Stevenson, Ellis, Melville and London
David Farrier

The Subject of Race in American Science Fiction
Sharon DeGraw

Parsing the City
Jonson, Middleton, Dekker, and City Comedy's London as Language
Heather C. Easterling

The Economy of the Short Story in British Periodicals of the 1890s
Winnie Chan

Negotiating the Modern
Orientalism and Indianness in the Anglophone World
Amit Ray

Novels, Maps, Modernity
The Spatial Imagination, 1850–2000
Eric Bulson

Novel Notions
Medical Discourse and the Mapping of the Imagination in Eighteenth-Century English Fiction
Katherine E. Kickel

Masculinity and the English Working Class
Studies in Victorian Autobiography and Fiction
Ying S. Lee

Aesthetic Hysteria
The Great Neurosis in Victorian Melodrama and Contemporary Fiction
Ankhi Mukherjee

The Rise of Corporate Publishing and Its Effects on Authorship in Early Twentieth-Century America
Kim Becnel

Conspiracy, Revolution, and Terrorism from Victorian Fiction to the Modern Novel
Adrian S. Wisnicki

City/Stage/Globe
Performance and Space in Shakespeare's London
D.J. Hopkins

Transatlantic Engagements with the British Eighteenth Century
Pamela J. Albert

Race, Immigration, and American Identity in the Fiction of Salman Rushdie, Ralph Ellison, and William Faulkner
Randy Boyagoda

Cosmopolitan Culture and Consumerism in Chick Lit
Caroline J. Smith

Asian Diaspora Poetry in North America
Benzi Zhang

William Morris and the Society for the Protection of Ancient Buildings
Andrea Elizabeth Donovan

Zionism and Revolution in European-Jewish Literature
Laurel Plapp

Shakespeare and the Cultural Colonization of Ireland
Robin E. Bates

Spaces of the Sacred and Profane
Dickens, Trollope, and the Victorian Cathedral Town
Elizabeth A. Bridgham

The Contemporary Anglophone Travel Novel
The Aesthetics of Self-Fashioning in the Era of Globalization
Stephen M. Levin

Literature and Development in North Africa
The Modernizing Mission
Perri Giovannucci

The Tower of London in English Renaissance Drama
Icon of Opposition
Kristen Deiter

Victorian Narrative Technologies in the Middle East
Cara Murray

Ruined by Design
Shaping Novels and Gardens in the Culture of Sensibility
Inger Sigrun Brodey

Modernism and the Marketplace
Literary Culture and Consumer Capitalism in Rhys, Woolf, Stein, and Nella Larsen
Alissa G. Karl

Haunting and Displacement in African American Literature and Culture
Marisa Parham

Haunting and Displacement in African American Literature and Culture

Marisa Parham

First published 2009
by Routledge
270 Madison Ave, New York, NY 10016

Simultaneously published in the UK
by Routledge
2 Park Square, Milton Park, Abingdon, Oxon OX14 4RN

Routledge is an imprint of the Taylor & Francis Group, an informa business

Typeset in Sabon by IBT Global.
Printed and bound in the United States of America on acid-free paper by IBT Global.

Library of Congress Cataloging in Publication Data
A catalog record has been requested for this book.

ISBN10: 0-415-99094-7 (hbk)
ISBN13: 978-0-415-99094-3 (hbk)

To the ancestors who seed,
the living who tend,
and my bean who grows.

What kind of case is a case of a ghost? It is a case of haunting, a story about what happens when we admit the ghost—that special instance of the merging of the visible and the invisible, the dead and the living, the past and the present—into the making of worldly relations and into the making of our accounts of the world. . . . It is not a case of missing persons sui generis, but of the ghost as a social figure. It is often the case of inarticulate experiences, of symptoms and screen memories, of spiraling affects, of more than one story at a time, of the traffic in domains of experience that are anything but transparent and referential. It is a case of modernity's violence and wounds, and a case of the haunting reminder of the complex social relations in which we live.

—Avery Gordon

All I know about music is that not many people ever really hear it. And even then, on the rare occasions when something opens within, and the music enters, what we mainly hear, or hear corroborated, are personal, private, vanishing evocations. But the man who creates the music is hearing something else, is dealing with the roar rising from the void and imposing order on it as it hits the air. What is evoked in him, then, is of another order, more terrible because it has no words, and triumphant, too, for that same reason. And his triumph, when he triumphs, is ours.

–James Baldwin, "Sonny's Blues"

Contents

Figures xiii
Permissions xv
Acknowledgments xvii

Introduction: Haunting and Displacement 1

1 Like Water: Hughes, Cullen, Johnson 13

2 "Do You Love Me?": *Another Country* 28

3 Behind Carma and Rosie 50

4 Folded Sorrows in Kaufman and Toomer 60

5 Saying "Yes" in *Kindred* 72

6 Winding Sheets: Petry and Wright 89

Coda: Future Expectations 106

Notes 115
Selected Bibliography 131
Index 139

Figures

1 Notorious B.I.G., *Ready to Die,* CD Cover Art. 4

2 James Van Der Zee, "Future Expectations (Harlem Wedding)," Gelatin silver print, printed 1974 [1926]. 113

Permissions

Empress Music Inc—Redwood Music Ltd. (Carlin), London NW1 8BD for the Commonwealth of Nations, Eire, Germany, Austria, Switzerland, South Africa and Spain in respect of the 50% interest in the Estate of Clarence Williams. All Rights Reserved. Used by Permission.

"The Negro Speaks of Rivers," "Danse Africaine," from *The Collected Poems of Langston Hughes*, by Langston Hughes, edited by Arnold Rampersad with David Roessel, Associate Editor, copyright ©1994 by The Estate of Langston Hughes. Used by permission of Alfred A. Knopf, a division of Random House, Inc.

"Poem," reprinted by permission from *This Waiting for Love*, by Helene Johnson, edited by Verner D. Mitchell, published by the University of Massachusetts Press, copyright ©2000 by Abigail McGrath.

"(What did I do to be so) Black and Blue," Words by Andy Razaf / Music by Harry Brooks and Thomas "Fats" Waller—©1929 (Renewed) EMI Mills Music, Inc. and Chappell & Co., Inc. All Rights Reserved. Used by Permission of Alfred Publishing Co., Inc. ©Redwood Music Ltd. (Carlin), London NW1 8BD for the Commonwealth of Nations, Eire, Germany, Austria, Switzerland, South Africa and Spain in respect of the 66.67% interest in the Estates of Harry Brooks and Thomas "Fats" Waller. ©Memory Lane Music for Australia, New Zealand, and United Kingdom (33.33%). Administered by Memory Lane Australia Pty Ltd (33.33%). ©J. Albert & Son Pty Ltd (66.67%) for Australia. All Rights Reserved. International Copyright Secured. Used By Permission.

"Rosie." Collected, adapted and arranged by John A. Lomax and Alan Lomax. TRO © Copyright 1934, 1946 (Renewed 1997 Ludlow Music, Inc., New York, NY). Used by Permission.

Acknowledgments

Like many things, this book took the long way, at times scenic, at others mainly detour. Usually it was both. But a great variety of people have assured its arrival, and I am fortunate to have so many people to thank. It is hard not to get too crazy with the thanks: I want to thank the grandparents who gave all for me, but also the sun that shined on the right days. I will do my best.

Yes, thank you to the family that has so encouraged me to pursue this dream, in Chicago and beyond. Thank you to the friends and professors who worked with me through the earliest versions of what is included here, Robert O'Meally, Ann Douglas, Andreas Huyssen, Dohra Ahmad, and Brian Hochman.

Thank you to the colleagues who really helped me push this project through to its end: Judy Frank and Karen Sanchéz-Eppler for their close-close readings; Jeffrey Ferguson, Prudence Cumberbatch, Andrew Parker, Andrea Rushing, and Jeffrey Stewart for their always on-the-ready encouragement; and my writing group at Amherst College—Rhonda Cobham-Sander, Hilary Moss, Marni Sandweiss, Martha Saxton, Lucía Suarez, and Martha Umphrey.

Thank you of course to the people who did all the millions of things that a book is never done without: Julie Howland for her meticulous attention to my very messy details, and my research assistant, Teana White, for her unflagging support and tireless feet.

And thank you, thank you, thank you to husband John and child Miles Henry. Where would I be without *those* thanks? Really?

Introduction
Haunting and Displacement

I started out believing that life was made just so the world would have some way to think about itself . . . Something is missing there. Something rogue. Something else you have to figure in before you can figure it out.[1]

—Toni Morrison, *Jazz*

If the readability of a legacy were a given, natural, transparent, univocal, if it did not call for and at the same time defy interpretation, we would never have anything to inherit from it.[2]

—Jacques Derrida, *Specters of Marx*

To describe an object or event as haunting is to latch onto something important about the meaning it gains in representation and circulation. "Nigger," from the mouth of a white person. Even casually, say from the mouth of a white friend repeating dialogue from a movie he has seen, or from the mouth of a white student reciting a passage from an assigned text. Despite knowing that the nigger is not meant for me, the event of the nigger nevertheless snaps me into a ghostly and uncomfortable relation with the speaker. My heart skips a beat, and, at least for a moment, I experience myself and the speaking other in a different way, as that mouth, at best loved and at worst neutral, seems suddenly tainted, something suddenly to be disavowed. Wrong word coming from the wrong mouth at what at the moment of utterance has become the wrong time. Brief shifts of scene, fleet shadows of performance: is the word's always haunting and surprising effect my burden or my privilege? Even when I expect its appearance, "nigger" unsettles me.

Once spoken, the word crystallizes as a site of memory; a span of cascading affects unfolds out of me at the word's utterance. Niggers, at least the ones conjured when I hear the word coming from the wrong mouth, are technically dead. They are assumed dead because it is assumed that the racist structures that engendered the term have already passed away, thereby removing the visible razor from the word's edge. Such assumption is motivated by a belief in forgetting, a belief that the dismantlings that serve as the best recognized valences of social and political progress—for instance Emancipation and the Civil Rights movement—were in fact complete demolitions, and that the relative absence of racism's visible structures signifies racism's absence. Afloat in the gap, how do I name the origin of my discomfort? By what instinct do I so immediately designate certain mouths as the right or wrong carriers of the word? Without a full, personal experience of the kind of event that would fulfill the word's material possibility, is my discomfort merely an echo of the past? And, if such is indeed the case, how do I account for what my body experiences in the depths of this discomfort? How do I relieve my suspicion, or my anger at being left to sift through the rubble, playing with things sharp and hard, yet ghostly? The moment passes. Nothing happened, but I remember.

Memory—conscious and unconscious, individual and collective—drives African-American cultural production in significant ways, and this book began as an ongoing consideration of the preponderance of elegiac objects in modern African-American literature and culture. Over time, however, it became evident that the kinds of memories I had become most interested in writing about were not always proper to the people who remembered them. Sometimes there may in fact be no recognizable origin for a memory, no single moment when a story was heard or a newspaper read. The remembrance itself might be no more than a feeling, a small start at a turn of phrase, a shiver at song's end. It is a feeling of something otherwise arriving from elsewhere, but that is nonetheless interpreted in the moment of its emergence as truthful and meaningful to personal experience: haunting.

In day-to-day speech, "haunting" denotes an evocation or experience of memory that is uncomfortable or unhappy, something bad that will not go away. But when one is faced with a bad memory, a funky, unruly memory, it is really just that, a bad memory. Now, if one were to experience someone else's funk, *then* one would be haunted. By giving name to the dreams and nightmares that come to us through each other's stories, haunting conceptualizes what it means for a person to have his or her *own* experience of another person's experience in the world. Someone might tell you, for instance, of a catastrophic event that he or she has experienced. A basic empathic desire might prompt you to declare: "I feel your pain," even as you know that this is not fully possible; you do not feel this pain. But how do you talk about the next morning, when, after a night of sweating through your own dream-versions of the story, you realize that despite your waking something has stayed with you, something has changed *about* you?

Haunting in its broadest sense is simultaneously a word for how knowledge comes together and also for how it breaks apart, a term for an experience that emerges at the crossroads between what we know well and what we do not know easily. In *Haunting and Displacement*, I work to elicit resonances within and between what I have characterized as narratives of encounter, displacement, and emergence. There are poems by Langston Hughes and Countee Cullen, conjuring and unraveling lost homelands, and James Baldwin's Rufus, slipping between the shadows and mirrors of race and gender, becoming a ghost, homeless and alone with watery blues. There is the haunting "oppositional nostalgia" of Jean Toomer's *Cane*, which as Nathaniel Mackey puts it, "wants to reach or to keep touch with an alternate reality as that reality fades," and the Beat poet Bob Kaufman, coming to terms with the "catastrophic histories buried" in his eyes. There is Octavia Butler's Dana, caught up in a web of uncanny synonymics, and James Van Der Zee's ghostly "Future Expectations," a collage photo in which the meaning of the present is brought into being through a haunting vision of the future.

The texts that appear in this book offer important ways of thinking through some of the relationships between memory, art, and the transmission of affect. In literary and cultural texts, haunting often appears as allegory, doubling, and irony. In its exploration of haunting and ghostliness, of phenomena of distancing and repetition, *Haunting and Displacement* pursues meaning in spaces wherein it has been made possible for people to testify to the effects of unwitnessed events or to understand themselves as subject to social and historical forces otherwise unnamed in a larger scene. Being haunted is by no means limited to African Americans, but, as we will see, the phenomenon is particularly important to understanding the persistent workings of memory and space in African-American literature and culture.

Haunting is not compelling because it resonates with the supernatural, but rather because it is appropriate to a sense of what it means to live in between things—in between cultures, in between times, in between spaces—to live with various kinds of doubled consciousness. It speaks to living not only with the sense that one's understanding of one's own social, political, or racial reality passes through other times, other places, and other people's experiences of the world, but also to living through those experiences in the very literal sense of *making it through.* When I think of being haunted, I remember back to my black friends and me calling each other "money," or my grandmother's always saucy and always appropriate, "nigga please." I think of the piles of chains, albeit gold chains, heaped around Mr. T's neck ("I wear these chains," he once said, "to show that I serve no one but me and God"), or the sweet brown baby on the cover of a favorite album, sitting atop the simple phrase, "Ready to Die" (figure 1).

At first glance, I simply see the *Ready to Die* cover image as signifying a cultural object to which I am attached, an album that I find pleasure in, both in its performance and also in the community to which knowing the album gives me access. With his big fluffy Afro and calm pose, set against the simple and clean scene—that is one cool kid. There is also, however, an explicit contradiction between the good feelings the cover evokes and its own openly-declared *raison d'être*, "Ready to Die." Even as my lack of discomfort marks my full immersion in the object's cool, there is something sinister in my complicity. Either I have chosen to let the image and its description remain separate, which signifies a splitting away from the full impact of the picture's reality, or I actually think it is okay to put

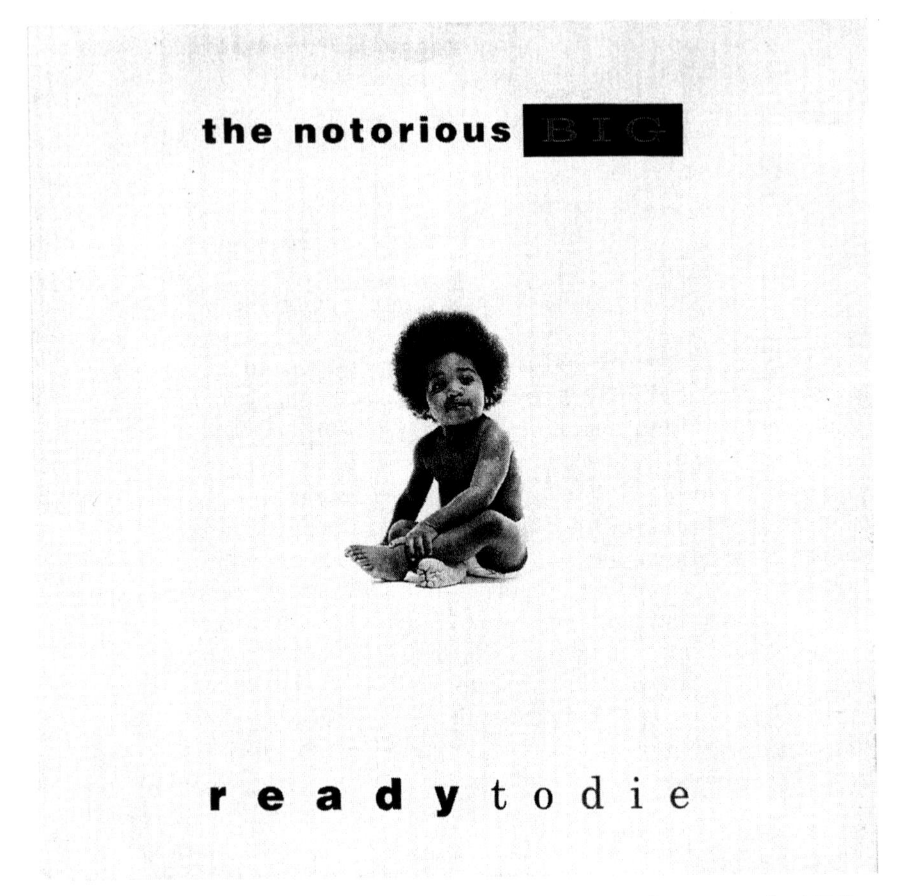

Figure 1 Notorious B.I.G., *Ready to Die*, CD Cover Art. (Bad Boy Records, 1994).

those words next to that child. Looking at *Ready to Die* now, on this page and away from its proper place in a stack of favorite CDs, I am unsettled. Something has shifted, and the sudden motion sickens me, makes me vulnerable to the emergence of the image's further implications, for instance the connection between the album's self-professed cool and the production of that cool in the shadow of black death and our expectations thereof. I suddenly see this image as a thing that should not be spoken aloud—much less reproduced. Taken alone, out of its milieu and in the quiet of contemplation, this image of the child becomes ghostly, horrible. As I think of this and other things, I feel myself at the edge of something. If the scene were to shift, I might imagine my friend on the auction block's steps and Mr. T's chains, now burdensome, become lead. It is a feeling that comes to me when I step into a Kara Walker installation and know what kinds of stories those shadow papers are asking me to admit to understanding. It comes to me on the street, every block written or painted with an R.I.P. or sketched "in loving memory of." Narratives without stories, ciphers for which I am the key; what *did* I do to be so black and so blue?

READING, I AND THOU

In their interpretive approach, the readings in this book rely heavily on evocation and allusion, a structural choice focused on eliciting submerged connections within and between texts, particularly texts that might otherwise not seem in address to one another. The chapters are arranged thematically, rather than historically across the twentieth century, with hope that loosening some of the historical relation might better illustrate how reading itself haunts and is haunted. To get at this, acts of reading and interpretation in this book are displayed as a kind of memory-work, which also highlights how our encounters with texts work on us, work us over, make us remainders of them. Dancing some of the boundaries between formalist critic, racialized and gendered reader, and cultural theorist creates a space in which texts might be engaged vis-à-vis their unexpected relations to one another.

This is not to say that mixing reader and critic does not bring its own problems. Reading asks for a collapse between reader and text, in the sense that to read is to dwell in the space of a text, to become beholden to its temporality, and it is from within the space of the text that we must come to love it or hate it, to need it or rebuke it. Interpretation, meanwhile, requires a particular kind of critical distance, as one's capacity to recreate the experience of being in a text from outside of that text requires communicating in a language that is often forcibly made foreign to the mainly subjective readerly self. But this critic who presents the text to her own audience has of course already herself been tainted by the aforementioned act of reading that initially prompted her interpretation in the first place. Much of this book is written from this tainted place so that haunting might emerge both as a method and as an object of inquiry, which is to say that the analyses in this text are often performative, working at, with, and through haunted strategies of reading. Authors' voices are carried across chapters, riffed and repeated, and shifts in my own use of first and third person are used to transition between displays of my touched and tainted reading and my larger interpretive concerns with form and the dissemination of meaning.

This decision to foreground the place and the play of different voices is also informed by the work of Saidiya Hartman, Dominick LaCapra, and other critics concerned with what Hartman has described as the "precariousness of empathy and the uncertain line between witness and spectator," which is a concern with what happens when one's desire to understand a victim's pain slips into a desire to feel and thereby know that pain, becomes what LaCapra refers to as "unchecked identification."[3] Such identification, even with the best intentions, could also be understood as an appropriation, appropriation often further complicated by asymmetrical power relationships between victims and witnesses. At the center of both authors' analyses is the question of how one places oneself in relation to a suffering other, and how that placement, even when most driven by compassion, risks also becoming a search for the self in the other. When that witnessed suffering is thus reproduced in the wake of such seeking, in the moment of that reproduction it becomes a story about the witness, as the person with whom the suffering began slips from view.[4] *Haunting and Displacement* is written with the assumption that there is much that always slips from view, and that knowing itself is mainly constituted as an interplay of vision and revision—of listening and remixing, and of finding ways, as Dori Laub puts it, to witness others while at the same time bearing witness to oneself in that listening, to thus also understand the self as "a battleground for forces raging in [oneself] to which [one] has to pay attention and respect."[5]

More generally, it is not the purpose of this book to suggest that all African-American experience can be reduced to my limited set of terms, for to do so would be to describe African-American life as a monolith. I am a specific person, singular in my interests and drives. But I am also a person who identifies with a subject position, African American, the progeny of American slaves—a subject position that has historically required that one understand at least a small part of oneself as beholden to the memory of others who share that position, as remembering often works in places of absence, for instance in lieu of homeland—or political power. In "Every Good-Bye Ain't Gone," James Baldwin speaks to this problem of boundaries between the self and others imagined as like oneself, which is a problem of identification. He arrives at the following conclusion:

> Some things had happened to me because I was black, and some things had happened to me because I was *me*, and I had to discover the demarcation line, if there was one. It seemed that such a demarcation line must certainly exist, but it was also beginning to be borne in on me that it was certainly not easy to find: and perhaps, indeed, when found, not to be trusted . . . [6]

Being haunted means struggling with things that come to us from outside our discrete experiences of the world, but which we nonetheless experience as emerging out of our own psyches. Such experiences trouble boundaries between self and other in their disintegration of boundaries between the personal and political. Much of my sensibility—my sense of active personhood, constantly propelled forward by my sense of personal truth—has been shaded in such ways. I feel pain, but have not suffered the blow. I have suffered other things, and now they are joined in my encounters, continuous, casting, shading, and signifying. Such a phenomenon, call it borrowing, intertextuality, or sampling, potentially empties out the term "memory"—or at least requires us to make more careful distinctions when considering the life of memory in the present, to think about what it means to be haunted.

ENCOUNTER, DISPLACEMENT, EMERGENCE

Haunting names how we experience the pain of others or, even more specifically, how the pain of others shades our own subjectivities. As a conceptualization of human relation that fundamentally depends on a sense of the individual, it also understands "individual" as a touched and tainted category, as captured in Stuart Hall's sense of the sociological self, or in Lacanian psychoanalysis' sense of selves who only come into being vis-à-vis their relations to others, through identification.[7] What is most compelling in Baldwin's take on the matter is the sense of process he has attached to his consideration of himself as both a person in a day-to-day sense, but also as a racialized, social subject consistently caught up in the twin dramas of self-making and disciplination, as a person constantly making meaning in the negotiation between whom we imagine ourselves to be and the requirements of who we must be in order to live in the world. That demarcation line is always moving, sometimes fast and sometimes slow.

In her 1988 novel *Beloved*, Toni Morrison offers up a theory of how memory circulates, how it crosses boundaries between people, how it haunts. Morrison's protagonist, Sethe, tells her daughter Denver why there is really no such thing as forgetting, explaining to her that "What I remember is a picture floating around out there outside my head." She continues:

> Someday you'll be walking down the road and you hear something or see something going on. So clear. And you think it's you thinking it up. A thought picture. But no. It's when you bump into a rememory that belongs to somebody else . . . The picture is still there and what's more, if you go there—you who never was there—if you go there and stand in the place where it was, it will happen again; it will be there for you, waiting for you.[8]

What Sethe refers to as her "rememory" blurs present and past, self and other, for at the conceptual center of rememory is the notion that our memories exist in excess of our own lives, that memories, "thought pictures," have attachments to the physical world that persist in our absence. Further, this movement is predicated on a slip between temporal and spatial registers—what begins as a narrative about time, about past and present, is here represented as also being about place. You can encounter this memory simply by being where it occurred, by stepping into the space indexed by that memory. Sethe's language in this passage is calm and explanatory, but on closer inspection, this slipping and blurring shows itself to be something quite troublesome, as if the unmooring that makes it possible for thought pictures to float away from their progenitors also loosens a series of other connections: what does one come to know in her encounter with a thought picture? What kind of responsibility might one have to this acquired knowledge? What does it mean to assume ownership over this memory, to "think it's you thinking it up?"

Sethe's description of rememory also depends on a problematic structure of address; much like the move from time to space, there is some slipping here between speaker and listener. In the passage above, Sethe's use of the second person begins innocently enough. It is at worst a Brooklyn-you, a "you" that functions as the storyteller's "I": *I am engaging you in a story about me by making you the same as me.* It is a common vernacular strategy, one that gives a story power by assuming that teller and listener are experiencing the story from a shared place: *you know what I mean?* Towards the end of the passage, however, this second person has become a little bit unruly, for not only are you required to possess something that is not properly yours, as you are reminded that you are a "you who never was there," but you as well may come to know that this thing that is not quite yours is "there for you, *waiting for you.*"

What begins as a convenient structure of address is revealed as quite strange and potentially creepy, and is itself grounded in an equally unusual temporal structure. The problem is not that this memory has agency, is waiting for you, but that there was in fact no you prior to this encounter. What at first seems a slip between time and place is thus revealed as a displacement, as you are made to know that that which constitutes you comes from elsewhere, and that it will come with or without your consent. It is there, waiting for you because "you," as the subject of this narrative, have only come into being at the moment of this encounter. What Morrison writes as a single-layered phenomenon—a narrative of encounter: you are walking along and bump into something—is thus revealed as multilayered, multidimensional: rememory is actually a story of a self unselfconsciously accepting the self in its arrival from another time and from another place. The bump does not precipitate movement back through time; it precipitates an unfolding, a movement back into the self and out again. However, because the first inward turn is largely unconscious, it is experienced as a repetition rather than as an emergence.

In this sense, that which is rememoried, the thought picture, is not the stable object Sethe's phrasing suggests. It is not like a rock on the ground, or a tree one might lean against. Rather, it is an experience of deep reflexivity, a narrative of ghostly and profound emergence that comes through some prompt. Upon encountering this prompt, information and intuition are collected together into something suddenly consistent, thus setting the stage for the emergence of a formerly nascent thing, for the larger meaning of the something heard or something seen with which Sethe's explanation began. Always and already waiting for you, every future encounter with that place will come to re-signify that first remembering: that which was not your own has become yours as you become responsible for its meaning in the present moment.

In *The Fire Next Time*, Baldwin writes:

> White people hold the power . . . and the world has innumerable ways of making this difference known and felt and feared. Long before the Negro child perceives this difference, and even longer before he understands it, he has begun to react to it, he has begun to be controlled by it. Every effort made by the child's elders to prepare him for a fate from which they cannot protect him causes him secretly, in terror, to begin to await, without knowing that he is doing so. . . . [9]

As with the slap young Sethe's own mother delivers to her when she asks her to "mark the mark," to brand her too, Sethe also imagines that she can keep Denver away from this horrible knowledge. She ends her description of rememory with an admonition to her daughter: "So, Denver, you can't never go there. Never. Because even though it's all over—over and done with—it's going to be there waiting for you." Here, Sethe's double negative belies the risk of her own storytelling, the power of which she desperately wants to displace onto the material site of the event. For Denver there actually is no going, only knowing, for place is not necessarily endemic to rememory. The danger she faces, however, is that of coming into being in a specifically historical epistemological space, a space in the self always haunted by the past. Knowing but not knowing—"Some things had happened to me because I was black, and some things had happened to me because I was *me*."

Some things had happened to me because I was black, and some things had happened to me because I was me: an African-American teenager might not immediately recognize the name "Emmett Till," but she might be more willing than a white classmate to see Raynard Johnson's suicide as a lynching. Raynard Johnson was an African-American teenager who in 2000 was found hanging from a tree in the front yard of his Kokomo, Mississippi home. The story made national headlines as questions emerged as to whether his death had resulted from a racially motivated crime—a lynching—or if it was in fact a suicide. Even as an autopsy pointed to suicide, interpretations of the event divided sharply along racial lines, with white townspeople more willing to accept his death as a suicide, and black townspeople, as well as his family, remaining unconvinced that Johnson's death—he had been know to date white as well as black women—was not in fact a "ghost of Mississippi." As a representative from The Southern Poverty Law Center noted at the time, "A hanging black man in Mississippi is a powerful thing that conjures up all kinds of images."[10]

And one can see how this conjuring is indeed a powerful thing, for conjures are not mere illusions. As Christopher Metress points out, there is something important to be learned "When Jesse Jackson senses the 'smell of Emmett Till,' when John Conyers feels the young boy's 'specter' rising from the waters of remembrance, when the citizens of Kokomo hear the echoes of Till's abductors in the barking dogs outside Raynard Johnson's house."[11] Smells, echoes, specters rising: the language used to describe such encounters points to the place of the fragment and affect in haunting, as small pieces of narrative suddenly and solidly come together to make meaning out of one's encounter with a site of memory. A conjuration is a collection of extant forces, collected into a meaningful and therefore powerful whole. What we see in the Johnson case, and what is also evident in a variety of such cases in the late twentieth and early twenty-first centuries, is that having a different understanding of the impact of the past on the present is endemic to racial difference in the United States.

Pleasurable or painful, an experience of haunting marks the return of something at once foreign and familiar: the feeling you get late at night, chancing upon a half forgotten song from some childhood basement-party, or when catching a whiff in the hallway of a neighbor's simmering pot. Haunting is the too mature fear a child experiences at the sight of a noose hanging from a tree in Louisiana, or a black college student who, having traveled to the South for the first time, looks up and cries out, briefly and suddenly imagining that some debris snagged in a tree after Hurricane Katrina is a body hanging, lynched. It is a feeling of resonance with a black voter's claim that she should not vote for a black presidential candidate because history has already written that he should die. As you will see in the coming chapters, *Haunting and Displacement* is structured around a series of such sites of memory.

The term *les lieux de mémoire* was popularized by the French historian Pierre Nora to describe constructed moments of memorialization that are not only condensations of symbolic meaning, but also tangible entities that operate in the absence of other sites, literally conjured *in lieu of* lost objects.[12] They are condensations, conjures, symbols. The smell of your neighbor's greens operates as such a site because the smell takes you back to another time and place; that simmering pot has status *as* a site precisely because you are no longer home—if you were at home, they would just be the same old greens. Sites of memory are particularly useful in considering representations of memory and haunting in black life because the term itself speaks to the sometimes beautiful, sometimes harrowing playfulness of haunting, a play rooted in slippages between and across time and space. Site/sight: where we put it, how we see it (or the myriad ways we see without seeing—hauntings, specters, and uncanny repetitions); site/cite: where we find it (the dig site, the grave, the Middle Passage), how we express it, or how loss informs or structures experience—citationality.

In regards to the work of haunting, *les lieux* are in *Haunting and Displacement* less significant as objects of historiographic inquiry, as at the center of a disciplinary concern, and are instead read in their significance to how the work of African-American artists itself theorizes an important interplay between space, memory, and haunting. As Lawrence Kritzman points out in his preface to Nora's *Realms of Memory*, a site of memory is "a polyreferential entity that can draw on a multiplicity of cultural myths that are appropriated for different ideological or political purposes." Writing themselves out of and into memory requires artists to find new ways of moving meaning across dimensions, across various representational, spatial, and temporal boundaries.[13] Limning the knowable and the lost, haunting is at once a metaphor for memory, a call to witnessing and a registrar of the distance between narrative and event.

FLOATING

What does it mean to live in this space? What does it mean to read about it, to write about it, or to name it a gift? In the final chapter of this book, which is about Richard Wright's *Native Son* and Ann Petry's "Like a Winding Sheet," I mention the 1919 Chicago riots, an event that deeply structured the relationship between race and space, segregation, in Chicago. The 1919 riot began with the death of a young boy named Eugene Williams, who was killed after inadvertently floating onto the wrong side of a segregated beach. Allan Spear, a noted sociologist and historian who penned the well-regarded treatise, *Black Chicago*, gives the following account:

> A seventeen-year-old Negro boy, Eugene Williams, drowned at the Twenty-Ninth Street beach in Chicago. The youth had accidentally floated across the unmarked barrier that separated the white and Negro sectors of the beach and had been stoned by angry whites. Nevertheless, the policeman patrolling the beach refused to make any arrests. Negroes, infuriated by the officer's indifference, attacked the whites, and soon the bathers were engaged in a pitched battle that rapidly spilled beyond the confines of the beach . . . For six days, white and Negro mobs terrorized the city, clashing on street corners, murdering passerby, and destroying property.[14]

As an adult, I have always found Spear's account of the riot compelling, if only because it gives official word to the stories that I had learned as a child growing up in Chicago.

I must admit though, *my* story is not quite the same story. I had been told that Williams had been stoned after he had accidentally backstroked into the cold, white waters. *He was so relaxed,* my Uncle Lebby once told me, *that he couldn't tell which way he was going . . . then pow!* Yet despite this difference in account Spears' story nonetheless speaks to my sense of what must have happened, for it has everything that means something to me: The purloined pleasure of the summer beach; the black child Sunday-floating along; an unmarked barrier between hostile nations; the stoning-death of an innocent. If you hold in your mind Chicago's history as a resolutely segregated city, then you might sense the epic qualities just beneath the surface of Spear's account, as its most difficult to quantify historical claim, Williams' ill-fated float, makes for a particularly instantiated metaphor.

Eugene Williams was not stoned by a group of whites after floating across an invisible barrier at a public beach. According to the official coroner's report, Williams died after unrelated fighting broke out on the beach between whites and blacks. Unable to hold on any longer to a tie he was using to keep himself afloat, and unable to come to shore because of the fighting, he drowned.[15] Witness testimony, meanwhile, offers still another story, that Williams and his friends were swimming at an isolated beach location, and that he drowned after being struck by a rock thrown by a lone white man, who had wandered away from the violence on the 29th Street beach, where a fight had broken out between blacks and whites.[16] What all accounts agree upon, however, is that when Williams' friends went to the beach patrol officer to report the crime, and pointed out its perpetrator, the officer refused to take action. The rest, generally, follows Spear's account. The riot lasted for days, spreading across the city and guaranteeing segregation's violent future in Chicago. The details of what had precipitated the riot, as well as its toll, were immediately mythologized as racial lore. The city coroner was eventually compelled to release a statement to the nation's public, asserting that there had in fact been only thirty-eight deaths during the Chicago Riots, not the thousands as "many people in and out of the city" believed was the case.[17]

I will not dwell here on the inconsistencies between the reports, for what I am interested in is what the reports share: It was a hot day; someone crossed a line; a boy died; there was a riot. My hearing is tainted. There is still something about Spears' account that won't let go of me. In it, despite my knowledge of the officially documented accounts, I still hear something that speaks to my sense of what must have happened that day. It is a desperate feeling, hearkening to everything I know about my world, bespeaking a certain cultural sensibility based in the meaning of historical losses both balanced and unbalanced against my particular experiences as an African-American woman. The boy's death prompts me to memory, for even if Spears' account cannot give me an objective truth, it still gives me something that must be remembered. *It was a hot day; someone crossed a line; a boy died; there was race riot. There was an innocent and then he was gone.*

1 Like Water
Hughes, Cullen, Johnson

> The past, to which we were subjected, which has not yet emerged as history for us, is, however, obsessively present. The duty of the writer is to explore this obsession, to show its relevance in a continuous fashion to the immediate present. This exploration is therefore related neither to a schematic chronology nor to a nostalgic lament. It leads to the identification of a painful notion of time and its full projection forward into the future, without the help of those plateaus in time from which the West has benefited, without the help of that collective density that is the primary value of an ancestral cultural heartland. That is what I call a prophetic vision of the past . . . [1]
>
> —Édouard Glissant

In "The Black Writer's Use of Memory," Melvin Dixon outlines some of the ways African-American writers have employed sites of memory in their work, calling on readers to reconsider the psychic and physical spaces we inhabit and how we use those spaces to complete various senses of group or individual identity. He is particularly interested in the way "Africa" became such a pervasive figure in twentieth-century African-American literature and culture, from figurations of the continent in Harlem Renaissance literature to the quite constant renaming of streets and neighborhoods in the 1960s and beyond. Dixon reads these practices as attempting to "enlarge the frame of cultural reference for the depiction of black experiences by anchoring that experience in memory—a memory that ultimately rewrites history."[2] He notes that,

> By calling themselves to remember Africa and/or the racial past, black Americans are actually re-membering, as in repopulating broad continuities within the African Diaspora. This movement is non-linear, and it disrupts our notions of chronology. . . . An investigation of Harlem as a northern urban community reveals direct—deliberate, crafted ties—to the American South and then to Africa. And these are not places but stages or sites on which the drama of self-acquisition is played.[3]

In Dixon's schema, a site of memory validates identity by anchoring a group's or individual's historically paratactic experience within a structure of meaning, thus retroactively inscribing such subjects into referenceable and narratable places in space and time. Such feats are by nature acquisitive, constantly calling real and imagined pasts into the service of the present.

Dixon's sense of "repopulating" and "re-membering" also hearkens to the pain of which Glissant speaks, another layer of loss coded in the black writer's obsession with the past's persistence. This obsession might be played out as a concern with space but that concern with space, with lost homelands and all that home signifies, also requires a narrative about remains, what it means to leave and what it means to be left behind. It is the problem of "the many thousands gone," a lamentation shaped in slavery and echoed today in the ceremonial libations performed in much contemporary African-American popular culture.

Perhaps at first the gone were the families and communities left behind in Africa; maybe later they were the ones who never survived the Middle Passage or the ones who died in slavery. Maybe they were families, friends, lovers, and children separated on the auction block or relationships fragmented by the scatter-effect of the Great Migration. Maybe they were the ancestors sacrificed to the exigencies of racial passing or, later, the black neighborhoods stunted by the deepening pervasiveness of urban blight. Indeed, on the facts alone, it might be reasonable to theorize the African-American community as one manifestly constituted through loss, losses that are often represented as migrations, as passages away. But, somehow, even as such a litany of unbearable losses carries more than a little something, it cannot carry everything. For even though "lamentation and mortification," as Karla Holloway puts it, have "both found their way into public and private representations of African America to an astonishing degree," with that tradition of loss also comes a tradition of "grace, hope, and resilience."[4] The losses may be unbearable, but, even sometimes paradoxically, they have been borne, and this despite the immense variety of physical and psychic violences put to making African arrivals in the New World as symbolically terrible as they were materially terminal. What we might come to realize, then, is that the term "migration" names a dialectic characterized at its poles by longing and innovation, by mourning and transformation. Becoming gone, in other words, is a process that transforms the lives of the people passing away and the lives of those who must come after. Every gone does not necessarily mean goodbye.

It is difficult to theorize migration's recoveries because it is difficult to imagine most kinds of afterlives, more so when we know that so many of the migrations forced and undertaken in the black diasporic experience have historically ended in death, terror, and destruction. But understanding recovery, understanding the fact that lives might again become livable after terrible events, is necessary to the interpretation of any art growing out of such events. The fact of writing after Middle Passage is particularly compelling when considered in light of the ways in which that journey might also be read as a journey out of subjectivity itself: from person to slave, from African subject to American commodity. In 1789, Olaudah Equiano would recount his own such journey from subject to object. Facing outward, towards the sea and away from home:

> The first object that saluted my eyes when I arrived on the coast was the sea, and a slave ship, which was then riding at anchor, and waiting for its cargo. These filled me with astonishment, that was soon converted into terror, which I am yet at a loss to describe, and much more the then feelings of my mind when I was carried on board. I was immediately handled and tossed up to see if I was sound.[5]

Standing at the threshold, Equiano sees the sea, which he describes as a "first object," adding "and a slave ship," as if the vessel were a mere accessory to the crucial first object, the site of the crime. Astonished by the alien ship, "waiting for its cargo," the newly enslaved African would not, even in retrospect, be able to find the language with which to express the quality of this terror. Being tossed announces the absence of speaking or agency, insofar as it presupposes the absence of personhood. Another captured African, Quobna Ottoba Cugoano, would write of his experience:

> When a vessel arrived to conduct us away to the ship, it was a most horrible scene; there was nothing to be heard but the rattling of chains, smacking of whips, and the groans and cries of our fellow-men.[6]

Metonymic, Cugoano's narrative sinks into passive voice as the scene's full implication comes to his reader in chains of sound and signification. Both men's descriptions move away from first-person, intensifying their descriptions of an intense breaking away at the genesis of a new identification:

> When I looked round the ship too [I] saw a multitude of black people, of every description, chained together, every one of their countenances expressing dejection and sorrow, I no longer doubted of my fate.[7]

Equiano's recognition of himself as the ship's cargo comes simultaneously with his recognition of other black people, people whom he, before this moment, would have had no reason to identify as black. Previously, if they were to at all be identifiable to him, it would have been through a series of other signifiers, through ethnicity, religion, language, and so on. Nor would he have had reason even to identify with them. Racial difference, as it were, was not a difference that mattered before Equiano's recognition of his own position within a new structure of meaning; his recognition of himself as a slave comes suddenly and through a nascent cognition of such difference. Like the sly permeation of saltwater through a coetaneous boundary, it is an awareness that assails the sensational body, drawing the boundaries of its imprisonment with sight, sound, smell, and touch. Forced to identify with the "black people, of every description, chained together," Equiano is put at a loss in his own transfiguration from an active, desiring subject into the object of an abject sentence. When Equiano steps onto the vessel and becomes the cargo, he enters into his new identity as a slave. He writes, "Quite overpowered with horror and anguish, I fell motionless on the deck, and fainted."[8]

In neither Equiano nor Cugoano's account is there a sense that any future could possibly follow those first moments of each man's enslavement. Their migrations are experienced as journeys into hell, and their stories narrativize processes of becoming one of the many thousands gone. Yet despite their descent into goneness, we also know that both men lived. Neither man would physically return to Africa, however, and the general absence of stories of return perhaps contributes to a historical sense of that first passage across the Atlantic Ocean as a movement across a critical and absolute boundary. Situated in both men's autobiographies as a state of freedom to which each slave must rightfully be returned, Africa becomes a figuration, a story of a stolen past told in the service of their political work as abolitionists. More than a century later, a young Langston Hughes would travel the world by ship, eventually crossing the Atlantic and returning to Africa, where he hoped to recover this past. The return, however, was not so easy, as the kind of ontological and spiritual recovery he sought would require more than landing on the soil of a land that had in fact been passed down to him as a figure. Ultimately, his journey to Africa may have been less satisfying than an earlier literary attempt, a metaphorical passage made possible through his exploration of a site of memory.

FLOWING

In the first volume of his autobiography, *The Big Sea*, Hughes recalls writing one of his best-known poems, 1921's "The Negro Speaks of Rivers." The poem was written during a time of relative despair, when, despite having both parents, he thought of himself as an orphan.[9] This sense of alienation is especially evident in his relationship to his father, a man with whom Hughes could not imagine identifying. In his autobiography, Hughes repeatedly remarks on this distance, often linking it to his father's "strange dislike of his own people," a dislike contrary to the younger Hughes, who claimed to trace many of his own best memories to working alongside other black people, mostly migrants from the South: "They seemed to me," he writes, "like the gayest and the bravest people possible—these Negroes from the Southern ghettoes—facing tremendous odds, working and laughing and trying to get somewhere in the world."[10]

When reading *The Big Sea*, and his later volume, *I Wonder As I Wander*, one cannot help but notice how Hughes spent much of his young-adult life in transit, which seems compelling in the life of a man whose artistic life work was so deeply invested in locking down the loci of African-American experience. Sitting on a train, on a journey to Mexico to meet his estranged father, Hughes has his first encounter with a site of memory, which he retells in the following way:

> Now it was just sunset, and we crossed the Mississippi, slowly, over a long bridge. I looked out the window of the Pullman at the great muddy river flowing down toward the heart of the South, and I began to think what that river, the old Mississippi, had meant to Negroes in the past—how to be sold down the river was the worse fate that could overtake a slave in times of bondage. Then I remembered reading how Abraham Lincoln had made a trip down the Mississippi on a raft to New Orleans, and how he had seen slavery at its worst, and had decided within himself that it should be removed from American life. Then I began to think about other rivers in our past—the Congo, and the Niger, and the Nile in Africa—and the thought came to me: "I've known rivers," . . . as the train gathered speed in the dusk, I had written this poem, which I called "The Negro Speaks of Rivers."[11]

Historically, being "sold down the river" did not always have to mean that one would actually take a trip down the Mississippi, yet even today the phrase nonetheless evokes a sense of irrevocable passage. During slavery it meant a trip to the auction block; today it still connotes deep betrayal. As a site of memory, the Mississippi may as well evoke the Atlantic, perhaps even a cultural memory of water as metonym for loss and separation.[12] But, in this passage, as soon as Hughes evokes the site's meaning, he immediately begins to recuperate it by pulling into his narrative the highly contested (though one would not think so here) story of Lincoln's journey down the Mississippi. By doing so, Hughes neutralizes the despair culturally attached to travel down the Mississippi, thus making it so that his narrative can instead end with slavery being "removed from American life." So openly recuperative; there is a sense here that the Lincoln story cannot quite align the end of the reminiscence with its beginning. But, nonetheless reaffirmed, Hughes is now able to recall "other rivers in our past," African rivers, followed by the realization: "'I've known rivers.'"

Hughes stages his final realization as an epiphany, as a revelation that has come to him via a journey back into his own memory, a journey I think we are supposed to understand as back into the self. This journey, he tells us, inspired "The Negro Speaks of Rivers," in which he draws an important relationship between blood and water, vis-à-vis the figure of the river:

> I've known rivers:
> I've known rivers ancient as the world and older than the
> flow of human blood in human veins.[13]

Antecedent to human experience is the fact of the river, the flow of which is here represented as ahistorical and outside the passage of human time. In this stanza there is an implicit similarity between water and the "flow of human blood in human veins," and it is through the construction of this identity-potentiate that Hughes is able to articulate a mobile and fluid subject, an enunciative "I" who has become as ahistorical as water itself. Indeed, if we understand Hughes as the "I" of the first stanza, as well as the Negro of the title, we can think of this poem as the Negro knows, and is therefore authorized to speak of, can tell others about, rivers:

> I bathed in the Euphrates when dawns were young.
> I built my hut near the Congo and it lulled me to sleep.
> I looked upon the Nile and raised pyramids above it.
> I heard the singing of the Mississippi when Abe Lincoln went down to New Orleans, and I've seen its muddy bosom turn all golden in the sunset.
>
> (5–10)

By positioning himself as the Negro of rivers, Hughes asserts his own timelessness as an experiential fact, particularly as this timelessness is made analogous to the lack of distance between the poem's geographical sites: read the river as blood, blood that flows across the landscape of time and space and through all Negroes. Within such a reading, the river signifies multiple I's that can be expressed as one. Such a reading also reveals the poem's heliocentric structure, as meaning radiates outward from the central set of images of the various rivers. This set at once describes and enables the multiple subject, an historically active I that attests to witnessing itself in its own past—*I bathed*, *I built*, *I looked*, *I heard*, *I saw*, I know—and thereby makes it appropriate for the poem to end with the moment of its own genesis. By returning the outer rings of its meaning to its center, the poem's structure becomes circular in three dimensions. Hughes watches the sun set over the Mississippi.

In the poem's denouement, "My soul" (13) stands as a universal soul that deepens with experience, and thus also points to an alternative way of reading the poem's title. On the one hand, to speak is to say, to tell of or to something actively: the Negro is the speaking subject. *To speak*, however, can also be interpreted as an adjectival gesture: the Negro "speaks of," as in reminds one of, bespeaks, rivers. In this second sense, "Negro" becomes a metaphor for "rivers," which authorizes the assertion "My soul has grown deep like the rivers" (13), and thus allows the speaker to graft onto a black collectivity a historical soul herein made continuous with his own, no-longer-problematic identity. In the discursive space of the poem, this soul recalls each episode as it witnesses itself across boundaries of time, space, and the Middle Passage. In his creation of a site of memory Hughes displaces responsibility for transcendence of the thetic onto water and thus transforms a site of historical loss into one of recovery, while nevertheless still carrying a trace of its original negative signification. Ultimately, the historical accuracy of each image in the poem's central stanza may be irrelevant as the text establishes itself as a *lieu de mémoire*, referenced to the racialized body: "And these are not places but stages or sites on which the drama of self-acquisition is played."

In *Revolution in Poetic Language*, Julia Kristeva insists that "the thetic conditions the possibilities of truth specific to language: all transgressions of the thetic are a crossing of the boundary between true and false."[14] If we understand the thetic as a term for a loss that cannot be recovered, in the sense that it is impossible for us to return to the world we occupied prior to desire, prior to language and the break that makes language possible, then to speak or write truthfully is to accept that limit: one only speaks of what one knows or sees, a constant and undying gesturing toward verisimilitude; anything else is only the product of an unselfaware imagination. The exception to this, however, lies in what Kristeva dubs "poetic language," a generative language that comes into being as the trace of an absence recognized or remembered vis-à-vis the semiotic.[15] She goes on to add that

> mimesis, in our view, is a transgression of the thetic when truth is no longer a reference to an object that is identifiable outside of language; it refers instead to an object that can be constructed through the semiotic network but is nevertheless posited in the symbolic and is, from then on, always verisimilar.[16]

Even though Hughes's place-names of course refer to material places, as sites of memory, Hughes's rivers are posited firmly in the symbolic and do not in fact exist outside of language. They are real and true places insofar as they exist to the subject, but false as they are not verifiable outside of an interpretative act, an act made possible only by the absence of the places themselves; again, in lieu thereof. With this poem, Hughes attempts to replace a racial past characterized by loss by diverting attention from the fact of that loss, even though it is the loss itself that engendered the text—and it is in this sense that the poem's citation of its constitutive absence reveals a fundamentally elegiac strategy, despite the recuperative elation with which the poem ends. Transformative in its symbolic turn, for it is in fact not a return, "The Negro Speaks of Rivers" is fully self-referential and self-authorizing in its attempt to tell us the truth about African-American origins and the veracity of black identity. It subverts notions of linear temporality, instead relying on repetition to convey a sense of constant, active flow, as if after the ending, "My soul has grown deep like the rivers," the poem could regenerate itself. In this way, Hughes imbues water with agency and represents it as the embodiment of perfect memory. Maybe, with time, the specific images would change—but the text, or rather its sub-textual energy, will always remain, beautiful and nostalgic, able to recast a moment in its most generative, therapeutic light.

On the one hand, to establish a site of memory commensurate with one's own body seems an efficacious strategy for overcoming the losses inherent to forced migration. Yet in its effort to overcome historical rupture and fragmentation, "The Negro Speaks of Rivers" produces a potentially haunting ideality, for the image the poem reflects back to its reader may exceed the reader's capacity to in fact meet the image and thereby experience the promise it offers. Further, insofar as successful identification relies on social ratification, Hughes's consciously racialized, homogenous site proves materially inadequate. The African American subject is by necessity a hybrid subject; for although there was not for Hughes a ratified identification with an ideal Americaness, for which we may hold responsible the racism of twentieth-century America, the fact of the Middle Passage nonetheless disallows an African American's identification as purely African.

Years after writing "The Negro Speaks of Rivers," Hughes would record in *The Big Sea* an attempt to attend a religious ceremony with Pey, one of his African shipmates. Hughes feels rejected when Pey does not identify him as African: "'But I'm not a white man,'" Hughes argues; "'You no black man, neither,' said Pey impatiently," thus rejecting Hughes's essentialized ideal of his own Africaness.[17] By doing so, by looking at Hughes and acknowledging difference, Pey exhumes the inescapability of the very thetic experience "Rivers" seeks to elide. Although he does not realize it, Pey removes the "African" from African-American and leaves Hughes with "-American": at a distance from American, not quite American, or simply a hyphen.[18] Pey relegates him to an ambiguous, heterogeneous space from which Hughes cannot claim a single, ratified origin. As Hortense Spillers has suggested,

> those African persons in 'Middle Passage' were literally suspended in the "oceanic," if we think of the latter in its Freudian orientation as an analogy for undifferentiated identity: removed from the indigenous land and culture, and not-yet "American" either, these captive persons, without names that their captors would recognize, were in movement across the Atlantic, but they were also *nowhere* at all.[19]

Pey's abjection returns Hughes to nowhere at all as he adds to Hughes's understanding of heritage a tacit awareness of his genealogical distance from Africa. As Arnold Rampersad notes, Hughes "quickly discovered that no African thought of him as one of them: 'The Africans looked at me and would not believe I was a Negro.'"[20] His, or for that matter any post-Passage subject's, desire to return to a pure, single origin is reasonable in light of the privileged status given to genealogical homogeneity in the context of any national identity. But the sanctity of the rivers, insofar as it posits an immutable racial origin, is undergirded by a misrecognition. Although

Hughes's water and blood metonym works in the interest of creating an unfragmented racial self, that same "blood"—genealogy—also reflects loss or, perhaps more precisely in this case, the truth of an heterogeneous, entangled origin, à la Hughes's own muddy Mississippi.

DAMMED

In what Dixon refers to as "an enigma of cultural memory," Countee Cullen's 1925 "Heritage" is everything "Rivers" is not.[21] It is as ambiguous as Hughes's poem is certain, something murky and sensate to the sun of Hughes's hot and hard self-affirmation. In "Heritage," one can never escape the absence of the thing itself, and here Cullen writes the lieu de mémoire as untenable. Soon after it begins, "Heritage" speaks its skepticism aloud:

> Africa? A book one thumbs
> Listlessly, till slumber comes.
> Unremembered are her bats
> Circling through the night, her cats
> Crouching in the river reeds,
> Stalking gentle flesh that feeds
> By the river brink . . . [22]

Here, the site of memory is self-consciously revealed as a site of artifice. This is captured in Cullen's figuration of Africa as a book, which, mindlessly perused, becomes the ultimate signifier of memory cut loose from its milieu, set adrift without context and without reference. The absence of an authentic site of reference makes unremembering possible, as the reader, or perhaps even the book's writer, actively chooses what to present. The imagery for what has been unremembered is sharp, dark, and quiet, as if the same river that brought Hughes a sense of comfort is for Cullen a place fraught with danger and ambivalence: there is no safety in Cullen's text. Further, if we continue the notion that sites of memory anchor experience, what becomes evident is that there is no anchor for a real body, for "gentle flesh," experiencing a real loss in the world, a loss that is not itself easily located.

As Dixon reads it, Cullen's poem "vacillates between acceptance and rejection of ancestry[;] the speaker's ambivalence fails to affirm—even ironically—the complexity of a self discovered through the art of memory."[23] But perhaps what Dixon identifies as a failure in Cullen's art is in fact the poem's organizing principle: this is a poem about the failure of art as compensation for reality, a failure that deepens the pain of remembering that one has unremembered something that one never knew. "Heritage" begins with a dilemma:

> What is Africa to me:
> Copper sun or scarlet sea.

Jungle star or jungle track,
Strong bronzed men, or regal black
Women from whose loins I sprang
When the birds of Eden sang
One three centuries removed
From the scenes his fathers loved,
Spicy grove, cinnamon tree,
What is Africa to me?

(1–10)

Where Dixon expects ironic self-reflection, Cullen offers tragedy, for even to write against the nostalgia of the constructed site of memory Cullen must use images gleaned from those very sites, a dilemma which is here played out as a problem of selection without knowledge: sun *or* sea, star *or* track, men *or* women. If "The Negro Speaks of Rivers," then, hearkens to the recovery of loss, "Heritage" moves inexorably towards the loss of loss. As recovery marks the emergence of the subject in Hughes's poem, in "Heritage" we instead find his dissolution.

The subject's dissolution is particularly compelling in light of what while reading the poem feels like the overwhelming presence of the speaker. The refrain, "What is Africa to me," has, by the end of the stanza, become "removed/ From the scenes his fathers loved," with no ostensible transition from the first to third persons. This transition, from *me* to *I* to *his*, and back to *me* again, makes suspicious the very notion of subjecthood. If one is removed from the scenes one's (fore)fathers loved, if one is detached from one's ancestry, what indeed does Africa as a site mean to the very notion of me-ness? What does this absence mean for one's very capacity for signification? And what, therefore, is the status of truth in the absence of reference? Is any utterance grounded in a *lieu de mémoire* necessarily untenable? The next stanza begins:

So I lie, who all day long
Want no sound except the song
Sung by wild barbaric birds
Goading massive jungle herds,

(11–14)

There are at least two possibilities of "lie": that he is lying, passive and immobilized by contradictory forces of presence and absence, and also that he is lying; he is not telling the truth. The act of lying is always characterized in this poem as an urgent response, strengthened here by Cullen's use of "So," which generates causality between the poem's stanzas. Gerald Early notes that

> Some readers have criticized "Heritage" for not offering more realistic images of Africa, decrying Cullen's ignorance, but that is one of the many levels on which the poem [works], the narrator is lying. These images of Africa are lies; certainly Cullen knew that. But is the poem also lying when it suggests that Africa means nothing to the narrator? Or is the poem lying when it suggests that African means anything to the narrator? Or is this very interiorized speech-act, speech-event poem nothing more than the system of lies that the impotent black intellectual uses to heal his own sickness of alienation and despair?[24]

Early is right to be suspicious, for is it not often the case that we suspect that a person claiming to have forgotten something is indeed lying? "I forgot" is different from "I never knew," for the former must compulsively offer up a trace of the supposedly disappeared. It must point to the site of the unremembered: "Something has gone missing, but I do not know how." Forgetting names a lost connection to a memory that may or may not still be present, and for this reason we might consider Cullen's lying as a way of positing memory's limit as analogous to a limit in representation: the distance implicit in any formally ironic or allegorical gesture, the representation of one thing as another, the act of naming without naming; such strategies reflect the constitutive contradictions of a person realizing that he has lost memory of an experience that he has never had but, nonetheless, needs. In its own way, Cullen's poem does everything Dixon would like it to do, but with unexpected results.

In "Heritage," Cullen offers us a subject about to explode under the pressure of balancing memory and history, and this is mainly articulated as a split between mind and body. The mind knows its history of absences and displacements; the body, meanwhile, is wrought by "pulsing tides" of memory (26). Like "Rivers," Cullen's poem represents a deeply self-referential experience, crossing boundaries between true and false by referring to nothing outside of the narrator's word. There is no truth but, and maybe more tragically, there is no false; he will not allow himself to be pulled into the book. However, unlike Hughes, whose poem disavows historical loss, Cullen interiorizes it, thus producing meaning through an incorporated contradiction, incorporated in the psychoanalytic sense, but also in the sense that Cullen makes the work of coping corporeal, leaving it to a body constituted by sensational acts of longing and un/remembering. In "Heritage," the narrator exists only as a tension between the history of himself in the world and what he experiences as his body's memory of something he has never known, a haunting affect.

In an essay entitled "The Site of Memory," Toni Morrison's notion of emotional memory speaks to this sense of remembering in the shadow of Passage:

> You know, they straightened out the Mississippi River in places, to make room for houses and livable acreage. Occasionally the river floods these places. "Floods" is the word they use, but in fact it is not flooding;

> it is remembering. Remembering where it used to be. All water has a perfect memory and is forever trying to get back where it was . . . It is emotional memory—what the nerves and the skin remember as well as how it appeared.[25]

Morrison begins her description with a disruption, the turning of the Mississippi River from its natural course. But because water has a perfect memory, because it cannot forget, it will always re-turn. Thus troped, Morrison's river offers her reader a kind of memory that operates on two distinct levels: as an image frozen in the mind's eye and as a sense that constitutes the body as a corporeal "I."

Such linkage to the past, however, is far from easy and, once recognized, exacts a cost. We might remember here that when rivers flood, homes are destroyed and lives are lost or displaced.[26] In "The Rhetoric of Temporality," Paul de Man notes that

> whereas the symbol postulates the possibility of an identity or identification, allegory designates primarily a distance in relation to its own origin, and, in renouncing the nostalgia and desire to coincide, it establishes a language in the void of this temporal difference. In so doing, it prevents itself from an illusory identification with the non-self, which is now fully, though painfully, recognized as a non-self.[27]

"Heritage" is haunted by the narrator's recognition of himself as the poem's subject, a subject who must answer to an unfamiliar and unrecognizable self that responds to calls he can never hope to know or understand. This haunting enables the poem's allegorical structure, insofar as the epistemological journey that carries him away from the constructed symbols that constitute his knowledge of Africa cannot in fact lead him to another alternative; there is only distance, embodied in himself. For this narrator, then, Morrison's flooding also means suffering from what he cannot know yet also cannot forget:

> So I lie, who always hear,
> Though I cram against my ear
> Both my thumbs, and keep them there,
> Great drums throbbing through the air.
> So I lie, whose fount of pride,
> Dear distress, and joy allied
> Is my somber flesh and skin,
> With the dark blood dammed within
> Like great pulsing tides of wine
> That, I fear, must burst the fine
> Channels of the chafing net
> Where they surge and foam and fret
>
> (19–30)

"Heritage" ends where "The Negro Speaks of Rivers" begins. In this instance, however, the river is dammed.

FLOODING

Although Cullen's poem focuses very clearly on the limits and dangers of the semiotic, it, in the end, also expresses the agony of a body that nonetheless threatens to attempt an impossible return. If we follow Kristeva, the presence-then-absence of the mother's body structures subjectivity, and thus our nature and will to participate in the symbolic—our very speech—flows and ebbs according to this loss. She refers to this as chora, antecedent to signification, felt as absence, and mediated by language—particularly as such absence is intentionally reified in poetic language—flowing through the subject and advocating the reclamation of lost sites. I hear this echoed in Morrison's claim that "Writers are like that: remembering where we were, what valley we ran through, what the banks were like, the light that was there and the route back to our original place . . . A rush of imagination is our 'flooding.'"[28] At the most basic level, thinking about memory vis-à-vis the semiotic offers a way of thinking about aspects of memory that often seem beyond interpretation yet are somehow always described. "Like water," Morrison concludes, "I remember where I was before I was 'straightened out.'"[29]

In a poem entitled "Danse Africaine" (1922), Hughes uses the figure of the drum to shift the responsibility for remembering more fully onto the body, which now must only respond to a prompt. Overdetermined, the rhythmic beating of the tom-tom moves the post-Passage body in time, moves it in memory of, in lieu of, the time before the break:

> And the tom-toms beat,
> And the tom-toms beat,
> And the low beating of the tom-toms
> Stirs your blood
>
> (12–15)

As long as the tom-toms beat, the post-Passage subject will respond to its rhythms. Unprovable, unreferenceable, and carried on the lowest frequencies, such notions, or perhaps more precisely such feelings—such surgings, such foamings, and such frettings—offer insight into the ways something familiar might be produced out of something we are never sure to know. But what, as Cullen might wonder, is the place of agency in this? Where is the balance between thinking one knows and knowing one knows?

Helene Johnson, another Harlem Renaissance poet, offers a sophisticated middle space between Hughes's acquisitive enthusiasm and Cullen's haunted weariness. In a piece entitled "Poem," Johnson speaks to how any ambivalence one might feel about a site of memory need not necessarily be antithetical to finding value or usefulness therein. The poem's speaker is a girl in a club, watching a singer on stage in Harlem:

> Little brown boy,
> Slim, dark, big-eyed,
> Crooning love songs to your banjo
> Down at the Lafayette—
> Gee, boy, I love the way you hold your head,
> High sort of and a bit to one side,
> Like a prince, a jazz prince. And I love
> Your eyes flashing, and your hands,
> And your patent-leathered feet,
> And your shoulders jerking the jig-wa.
> And I love your teeth flashing,
> And the way your hair shines in the spotlight
> Like it was the real stuff.[30]

There is obvious affection in her references to the performer as "Little" and "Slim" and "big-eyed," descriptions that might seem otherwise incongruous with his status as an entertainer at a one of Harlem's most important night clubs. And it is indeed clear that, despite the quiet "gee, boy" intimacy with which she describes him, he holds her too in his power:

> Gee, brown boy, I loves you all over.
> I'm glad I'm a jig. I'm glad I can
> Understand your dancin' and your
> Singin', and feel all the happiness
> And joy and don't care in you.
>
> (14–18)

Here, the speaker's identity as a jig comes into being through her sense of understanding the brown boy's performance. On stage, he is visually enlarged and vibrant, "flashing" and "jerking" and shining. But, again, there is something slow and drawn-out in her description of him, and this slow-motion tempo creates a sense that the speaker might somehow know more about the boy on stage, in his presence, than the poem's reader ever could. Perhaps this is because even though the poem's imagery gives us one thing, a bright, fast, and vibrant jig-wa, the poem's speaker distinctly hears something else behind the visual, something moving on a different time:

> Gee, boy, when you sing, I can close my eyes
> And hear tom-toms just as plain.
>
> (19–20)

"Tom-toms"—a new buzzword to the Harlem Renaissance, a newly enlarged frame of reference, a still-fresh site of memory that refers back to the "dancin'" and the "Singin'" and "the happiness." Does she hear the tom-tom in his voice? Or does she hear the tom-tom in her own listening?

> Listen to me, will you, what do I know
> About tom-toms? But I like the word, sort of,
> Don't you? It belongs to us.
>
> (21–23)

The speaker hesitates in the midst of her reverie. She knows that, despite the real pleasure she might experience in her feelings, there might also be something superficial, artificial, in hearing tom-toms behind his voice. But what matters is the ownership and sharing of the artifice, more so than the relative veracity of its significations. After this brief hesitation, the poem ends by echoing its own beginning, now even further collapsing the distance between the speaker and the boy on stage:

> Gee, boy, I love the way you hold your head,
> And the way you sing, and dance,
> And everything.
> Say, I think you're wonderful. You're
> Alright with me,
> You are.
>
> (24–29)

The distance is closing, but not completely. Much as the singer's hair shines in the spotlight only *like* "the real stuff," there will be no grand becoming or explosive transcendence. She does not become him and he does not become anything more than who he already is, a boy with a banjo. "You're / Alright with me," is not even "I love you." But it is a real affection. And what matters here is the graciousness of the final "You are," all anyone needs to give and receive in order to live life more fully, the final purpose of any site of memory.

2 "Do You Love Me?"
Another Country

> It was Bessie Smith, through her tone and her cadence, who helped me to dig back to the way I myself must have spoken when I was a pickaninny, and to remember the things I had heard and seen and felt. I had buried them very deep. I had never listened to Bessie Smith in America (in the same way that, for years, I would not touch a watermelon), but in Europe she helped to reconcile me to being a 'nigger.'[1]
>
> —James Baldwin

At the end of the previous chapter, I made the claim that the speaker's identity in Helene Johnson's 1927 piece, "Poem," is explicitly tied to the space in which and with which the identification is made. The poem is set "Down at the Lafayette"—the Lafayette Theater, one of Harlem's most well-known venues for live performance—and it is written from the perspective of a young woman in the audience, watching a banjo player on stage and feeling caught up in the thrall of his performance. "Gee, brown boy," she tells him, "I loves you all over./ I'm glad I'm a jig. I'm glad I can/ Understand your dancin' and your/ Singing . . .".[2] The speaker's identification of herself as a jig places her socially, racially, and sexually within a particular milieu. Yet even as she cites her identity as a reason for why she understands this boy whom she does not know, one also gets a sense that it is her encounter with him in the time and place of his performance that has brought this identity into being in the first place. There is a small gap, then, between the fact of this encounter—they are anonymous to each other—and her reception of it, which Johnson writes in close and intimate terms. Indeed, it is impossible to read the poem outside of this intimacy, which leads us to imagine that, despite all exigency, in this moment this girl gets it, and she gets it like she's always got it.

Out of this gap a second thing appears, as she hears something else in the performer's presence: "Gee, boy, when you sing, I can close my eyes/ And hear tom-toms just as plain" (19–20). In the previous chapter's reading of the poem, I took Johnson's poem as an example of how we create sites of memory to create community, over and beyond the veracity of our relationships to the objects used as the signifiers of that community: the speaker might not be sure what a tom-tom is, *per se*, but she can know that she hears it because the word itself had by that time come to have particular meaning to 1920s Harlem, a meaning that was located *in* and was also *about* Harlem—again, even as the representation of that meaning was displaced onto the African drum as its signifier: "Listen to me, will you, what do I know/ About tom-toms? But I like the word, sort of,/ Don't you? It belongs to us" (21–23).

"There are *lieux de mémoire*," Pierre Nora tells us, "because there are no longer *milieux de mémoire*, real environments of memory."[3] This "real environment" that Nora claims as lost was an essentially pre-modern, pre-migration world where tradition and emplacement engendered and enriched living. It would never be necessary to turn to the past for meaning, because meaning was always present in milieu:

> If we were able to live within memory, we would not have needed to consecrate *lieux de mémoire* in its name. Each gesture, down to the most everyday, would be experienced as the ritual repetition of a timeless practice in a primordial identification of act and meaning.[4]

In this world, simply being accomplished what would by necessity later be overtaken by remembering. *Les lieux*, then, are objects constructed as replacements for experiences one would have otherwise experienced as part of a milieu, and it is the purpose of these objects to reconstruct for their beholders the sensibilities and sensualities of lost worlds, to generate a sense of meaning bridged by affect. Even though sites of memory are often represented as objects—Proust's tea-softened madeleine, the play of sun on a face, the crunchy sweetness of Baldwin's watermelon—one's encounters with such objects prompt brief returns to lost times, times that have in retrospect been made continuous with lost places, places *themselves* now inseparable from one's specific way of experiencing oneself as a person in a world. It is thus useful to characterize these prompts precisely *as* sites because they open up for the beholder a realm of memory that is fundamentally spatial, a time remembered on the level of affect as an occupancy: what it felt like to be some*where*, more so, even, than to be back in some*time*. In such *milieux de mémoire*, there is no "past." There is only the present as it is conjured in moments of relation, a phenomenological contingency.[5] In this sense, real environments of memory are no more based in concrete spaces, in geographical locations that one could point to on a map, than memories are bound to recollection. They are abstracted, conjured spaces, beholden to the kind of intersubjectal magic empathy works.

I think of magic when I sense that I am feeling an experience in a way that exceeds the general theoretical limits of such an experience. The sensation of this truth is difficult to reproduce, and the closest I can come is the feeling of being in a club or at a party, and a certain song comes on, is *put on*, by a DJ with perfect timing. At that moment, certain people with certain things in common will come to attention, each with a certain look on his or her face. Each feels something, and if one of these people were to catch the eye of another of these people, without really knowing each other they would nonetheless *know* something about each other and about themselves, generating in the space between a real environment of memory, an environment bolstered by this interplay of insiders and outsiders, by a sense of constitutive knowledge consolidated in the moment of experience and bolstered by the sense of having come from another place. This is what Nora is getting at when he asserts that while history is tied to time, memory is tied to space, to habitus. A roll of the eyes, a hand on a hip, a cooking smell, rhythm, a spray of salt water: This thing Nora has put in the place of "collective memory," is a sense of memory tied to having a way, to having a certain kind of cultural sensibility.[6]

Much like that which Morrison articulates as rememory in *Beloved*, *les milieux de mémoire* are constructed more of shared feelings than of literally shared experiences. As explored in the introduction to this book, one can imagine that this thing that allows meanings to go unspoken between compatriots might thus also allow the sharing of things otherwise unexpected, but nonetheless recognized upon their arrival. Taken together, the object-space Nora describes as a site and the process of encounter and emergence Morrison refers to as rememory together describe one's experiences with geographically mobile and temporally redolent structures of shared feeling that make possible one's capacity for sudden shifts into common understandings of fleeting, conjured relations. In this sense, then, memory has less to do with the past and its representations and everything to do with a group's ability to use a shared representation to comprehend an event vis-à-vis its meaning in the present.

BLOWIN'

Even though memory, as I have posited it above, conjures abstract space, in speaking of the relation between space and memory it should be understood that this conjured space can still have a relation to the concrete, insofar as "concrete" refers to a material place of safety, a place where one can feel ready to feel. In James Baldwin's 1962 novel *Another Country*, jazz clubs constitute the central habitus for an artists' milieu that imagines itself as apart from the rest of the world, operating in stark comparison to its outside.[7] Baldwin introduces us into this world through Rufus, a young, hip, and black jazz musician living in 1950s New York, playing the big clubs at night and spending his days with a racially diverse group of fellow artists, including his best friend, a white author named Vivaldo.

Rufus' life constitutes the first third of *Another Country*, his story beginning moments before he commits suicide off the George Washington Bridge and ending with his funeral. Baldwin's decision to begin telling Rufus' story from its end directs the reader to look for what might have brought him to the book's inaugural death. The book's epigraph, "You took the best, why not take the rest," the refrain from Billie Holiday's "All of Me," also pushes reading in this direction. Lyrically, "All of Me" welcomes self-disintegration in the wake of lost love. When the love-object leaves, the body is ironically revealed as only valuable as a mechanism of attachment to another—arms that hold, lips that kiss—and is thus revealed as only itself having meaning as it is loved, as having meaning only in its heart, which in the song is expressed as a space inhabited by he or she who is loved, now lost. "The best" that is taken is the self, because the self is nothing but that which has been vested in it by another. In "All of Me," after love is gone all that is left are eyes, eyes only used, we are told, for crying. What used to be the site of correspondence, of revelation of the self and absorption of the other, instead becomes the site of loss, salt water.

In *Another Country*, Baldwin stakes the moral, emotional, or ethical meaning of every relationship on the possibility for lasting attachment, a phenomenon that itself depends on successful communication across the space between people who have themselves only come into being through other, prior, attachments—attachments that may or may not be comprehensible to others outside of that past, real or conjured. After all, if we imagine "memory" as a word for relation, what are the possibilities for or constraints on relation if that remembering cannot be shared, if that place cannot be entered into? How might any two people come to terms when they hear the words differently? What does this mean for difference more generally, for loving across any experience—experiences themselves haunted by prior, often willfully forgotten, attachments? By pushing readers through a long series of temporal and spatial collapses, as experienced by the novel's many characters, Baldwin offers a rigorous exploration of how experiences of race, sex, class, and gender constantly and fleetingly come together and fall apart.

Rufus, the novel's own best thing, suffers greatly in the muddy roil between these powerfully divergent and convergent forces and, ultimately naive to the power of other people's obdurate forgetting, dies. Rufus is particularly susceptible to destruction because, according to Baldwin, he is the first of the novel's characters to realize the extent to which his self-meaning is constituted by others. He comes to this through his relationship with Leona, a Southern white woman. Outside of the jazz club, he is forced to recognize "the big world" that "stared unsympathetically out at them from the eyes of the passing people." Rufus—despite growing up in Harlem, traveling the world in military service, and living a rough and glamorous life as a popular uptown/downtown jazzman—thus encounters his own naiveté, realizing that "he had not thought at all about this world and its power to hate and destroy." Baldwin stages this destruction both structurally and thematically, for instance describing "the big world" coming "out at" Rufus and Leona "from the eyes of the passing people." By removing agency onto the mechanism of its transmission, having the eyes rather than the people doing the seeing, Baldwin touches on the power of the social to take possession of and to speak through its subjects, an interdiction that allows people to judge others without taking responsibility for what that judgment or its meanings might wreak. Again the eyes become the site of loss, as the possibility for attachment, the love of the other, is foreclosed at the moment of looking.[8]

Later, after his relationship with Leona has been destroyed and he has become broke-down and alone, Rufus' distance from others kills him. Baldwin blames his disintegration on the world, stubborn and childish in its resolute apathy:

> Entirely alone and dying of it, he was part of an unprecedented multitude. There were boys and girls drinking coffee at the drugstore counters who were held back from his condition by barriers as perishable as their dwindling cigarettes. They could scarcely bear their knowledge, nor could they have borne the sight of Rufus, but they knew why he was in the streets tonight, why he rode subways all night long, why his stomach growled, why his hair was nappy, his armpits funky, his pants and shoes too thin, and why he did not dare to stop to take a leak.[9]

In *Another Country*, Baldwin's narrative voice is as intimate with the world as it is with his characters, and it soars when they are one and the same, bringing together his fictional and nonfiction writing. It is the voice of indictment and authority, unwilling to stop until everyone pays for the death of a protagonist whom he lets loneliness kill in the novel's first hundred pages. The "they" here extends past the anonymous faces on the street to each of the novel's characters, and then on to each of the various novels and songs the characters themselves create: to his friends, Richard's novel seems a cold failure; Vivaldo feels incapable of knowing his novel's characters. "They could scarcely bear their knowledge, nor could they have borne the sight of Rufus, but they knew. . .". Throughout the novel Baldwin cites apathy, the forced absence of affect, as the *modus operandi* of the novel's many walking dead. They cannot bear the sight of Rufus because to do so would require recognizing the possibility of themselves in Rufus. Empathy (again, for better or for worse), elicits identification. Apathy, meanwhile is the trace of identification's refusal, a refusal of knowledge that, in *Another Country,* is articulated as a kind of death. At Rufus' funeral, the preacher declares: "If the world wasn't so full of dead folks maybe those of us trying to live wouldn't have to suffer so bad."[10] Rufus is Baldwin's sacrifice, a ghostly figure around whom social meaning has been collected and contained.

Before he dies, Rufus cannot bear the sight of himself. Standing empty and poor outside his former jazz-haunt, Rufus remembers an empathic experience, a moment of feeling fully within his sensibility. He remembers being inside the club the night "he came doubly alive" when his band's saxophone player "took off on a terrific solo. He was a kid of about the same age as Rufus, from some insane place like Jersey City or Syracuse, but somewhere along the way he had discovered he could say it with a saxophone. He had a lot to say."[11] Despite the circumstances of his life, a life away from, Baldwin notes, "the city," the saxophonist still finds jazz, a language with which he can translate his troubled past into art. If one were to pursue this from a psychoanalytic perspective, one could theorize this function of jazz in Baldwin's text as primarily one of introjection, as a transformative process. In *Another Country*, Baldwin mainly uses the figure of the saxophonist, however, to exemplify the identity that Rufus has lost, an identity made plausible by the spaces he once inhabited. It is a glimpse of who he has un-become, and Baldwin's prose accelerates as "He," the saxophonist,

> stood there, wide-legged, humping the air, filling his barrel chest, shivering in the rags of his twenty-odd years, and screaming through the horn *Do you love me? Do you love me? Do you love me?* And, again, Do *you love me? Do you* love *me? Do you love* me? This, anyway, was the question Rufus heard, the same phrase, unbearably, endlessly, and variously repeated, with all the force the boy had.

If this were a song, the question would make the refrain as the verbs set the tempo: *humping*, *filling*, *shivering*, and *screaming*. Baldwin makes sure this music is audible, using repetition and variation to generate, on the surface of the text, the closest he can come to a jazz riff. The first set of repetitions is exactly that, repetition; its power continues out of the verbs leading up to the moment of reiteration, again the *humping*, *filling*, *shivering*, and *screaming*: "*Do you love me? Do you love me? Do you love me?*" The question, *do you love me?*, forefronts what is to Baldwin the fundamental problem of human relation, as love must always hang between empathy and identification. Love, like haunting, marks an affective third space of relation: to love me is to care for me as unconditionally as you care for yourself, even as you know that I am not you, and never will be. Love is the other country, the other space of being. (Later, Vivaldo wonders how he and Ida had "remained so locked away from one another?" Baldwin, at the height of his omniscient and ominous narration explains, "Love was a country he knew nothing about.")[12] Complication—variation—comes as italicization in the second set of repetitions, which marks the deepening and widening of the primary theme. "Do *you love me?*": Are you sure you love me, really? "*Do you* love *me?*" As the only variation where the change in textual emphasis actually alters the meter, it carries the big question: You might like me, but do you even know what *love* is? And then, finally, a return to the thematic root: "*Do you love* me?" Readers should also hear in this a future echo with what, in *Song of Solomon*, Toni Morrison refers to as "what all human relationships boiled down to: Would you save my life? or would you take it?" These questions, which emerge as a description of Milkman and

Guitar's simultaneous love and rivalry, make visible the fine line hovering between the living and the dead, and are grounded in the moment at which that line is understood as in the hand of another, for it is also a question about our responsibilities to the lives of others.[13]

Do you love *me?* In *Another Country*, the force of this question, striking and elemental, shakes the audience, wakes the dead as

> The silence of the listeners became strict with abruptly focused attention, cigarettes were unlit, and drinks stayed on the tables; and in all of the faces, even the most ruined and most dull, a curious wary light appeared. They were being assaulted by the saxophonist who perhaps no longer wanted their love and merely hurled his outrage at them with the same contemptuous, pagan pride with which he humped the air.[14]

Would you take my life or would you save it? The line between dissipates with every blow of the saxophonist's horn, and the audience can feel something happening. However, despite the "contemptuous pagan pride" of his performance, we must remember that the question comes from a fundamentally broken place. *Do you love* me? And this is one reason why, by the end of *Another Country* the reader will come to understand how she was supposed to see something special in the audience's rapt attention to this boy's blows, for as Baldwin would assert later in the novel, most people live their lives in fact avoiding the recognition of the blows they have themselves suffered, avoid tending to the ways in which they, too, are broken:

> The occurrence of an event is not the same thing as knowing what it is that one has lived through. Most people had not lived—nor could it, for that matter, be said that they had died—through any of their terrible events. They had simply been stunned by the hammer. They passed their lives thereafter in a kind of limbo of denied and unexamined pain.[15]

Abrupt and total, it seizes them as the light in their faces symbolizes their growing recognition. It must necessarily be a wary light because this coming into knowledge brings its own ethical requirements. The audience is suspended between the listener's intuition—a nascent empathy that is a kind of knowing—and really *knowing* what they know. This tension captures Baldwin's always ironic sense of racial redemption as that which remains unattainable because people fear love, love that, in Baldwin's universe, represents empathy's highest calling, knowledge on the lowest frequency—*knowing* that you *know*.

In the jazz club, caught in the magic of the space that the saxophonist, this boy, has helped conjure, the audience has no choice but to know, thus making this one of the rare moments in the text when communication actually chances success:

> the boy was blowing with his lungs and guts out of his own short past; somewhere in that past, in the gutters or gang fights or gang shags; in the acrid room, on the sperm stiffened blanket, behind marijuana or the needle, under the smell of piss in the precinct basement, he had received the blow from which he never would recover and this no one wanted to believe. *Do you love me? Do you love me? Do you love* me?[16]

Any sense that the boy's blowing refers to a single event is undercut by the instability of reference in the passage: "gutters *or* gang fights *or* gang shags"; "marijuana *or* the needle" (my emphasis). It is precisely this lessened specificity, however, that opens the boy's music to the audience. There is a sense that the audience gets it, as signified in their "abruptly focused attention." The boy's blows demand recognition for other blows, blows unlike the expressive act in which he is engaged, but that can only best be communicated through another kind of blow. This is particularly important in light of the tone in the passage reproduced above, which is heavy with smell, with its unstable reference gesturing as much toward an inarticulability of experience as toward a sense of shared experience. For Rufus, the solo is the apotheosis of communication. Maybe the boy is expounding on some other pain, but this question: *do you love me?* is the only answer to that pain, whatever it may be. Rufus cannot "know" what the saxophonist is saying, in the sense of knowing the specific thing that has brought him to his solo. Yet, despite the singularity of each of their experiences, Rufus can nonetheless *know*. Maybe, for the saxophonist, there was no gang, there was no blanket, there was no weed and there was no needle. Rufus can be sure, however, that there *was* a blow, and he knows it because he too has suffered it. No one else wants to believe it, however, because the saxophonist is a boy, "a kid," "shivering in the rags of his twenty-odd years," and speaking a long pain "out of his own short past." What does it mean for him to be broken? "*Do you love* me? This, *anyway*, was the question Rufus heard" (final emphasis mine).

Hours before his own death, Rufus remembers how he felt accompanying the saxophonist, *able* to accompany because he understood, and it is by virtue of his understanding that Rufus feels himself as part of the music: "The men on the stand stayed with him, cool and at a little distance, adding and questioning and corroborating, holding it down as well as they could with an ironical self-mockery." The band stays cool, as anyone would try to when another is telling his or her story, preferring to appear as the interpreters of the story, rather than as its protagonists. Their cool, however, is a front, because "each man knew that the boy was blowing for every one of them. When the set ended they were all soaking." The song is the prompt, and its effect is real as everyone untouched by the spirit of the moment has become a foreigner, a *milieu*.

Milieu, a real environment of memory composed not of shared events, but of a shared recognition of the past's tenor, enables an elicitation of the shared recognition of an event's meaning. Rufus' knowing, his identification with the saxophonist, gives Rufus his meaning, and on a textual level this articulates his status as jazz's manchild. Knowing yet not-knowing breaches the gap between self and other. This knowingness, this connection in the past, is a magical knowledge that comes without details, a "primordial identification" which by the twentieth century had become an aesthetic experience of an episteme. The listening constructs not only the knowing, but a nascent understanding of how one has come to know.

BLACK AND BLUE

Beyond the scenes of music-making endemic to Rufus' status as a jazz musician, jazz and the blues suffuse Baldwin's novel, beginning with the blues traveler-title of the novel's first section, "Easy Rider," to the Billie Holiday and Bessie Smith lyrics interwoven through that section as well.[17] In Baldwin's writing of Rufus' fall, blues lyrics soundtrack the workings of identification between Rufus and other characters, giving contour and texture to the explicit connections Baldwin has already established between memory, knowledge, and experiences of listening in *Another Country*. In this text, music bridges, and thus offers an important metaphor for human relation, for how knowingness flows away from the self and back again. In their thematic appearances, Baldwin's lyrics crystallize an affect generated in a given scene, gathering into Smith's "Jailhouse Blues," "Empty Bed Blues," "Backwater Blues," and Holiday's "All of Me" an emotional energy that also sets the conditions for bringing the implications of otherwise specific events into larger fields of meaning; again, milieu. Structurally, however, these same lyrics work to an opposite effect, instead highlighting how a person's interiorization of a text's meaning might also foreclose communication across racial, gender, and social difference. Like an evocation of memory or the subtle movement of sensation across a body, an act of coming to know is largely invisible to anyone outside of the experiencing body, a body prompted in and by the presence of an unknowing other. In this contrast between music as structural or thematic element, then, Baldwin offers a striking commentary on how even a most full or fulfilling experience of sharing, of being together, listening together, sexing together, might also set the condition for a more profound separation, as coming to know the limit of a shared experience can bring something more empty and alone than even loneliness itself.

The night of his suicide, after Leona had been taken back South and before he found himself standing outside the jazz club, Rufus had come into a new kind of knowledge, one consecrated by the blues. While sitting together in Vivaldo's apartment, Rufus and Vivaldo drink over Bessie Smith. Rufus has been missing for weeks, living on the streets, and is trying to explain to Vivaldo how such a thing could happen, especially to *him*. To fill the uncomfortable silence risen between them, Vivaldo, a white hepcat writer and Rufus' best friend, has put on the A-side of Smith's groundbreaking 1927 album, *Backwater Blues.* They sit in silence, listening to the title track. Though they are listening to the same song, what each hears is quite different:

> *There's thousands of people,* Bessie now sang, *ain't got no place to go,* and for the first time Rufus began to hear, in the severely understated monotony of this blues, something which spoke to his troubled mind. The piano bore the singer witness, stoic, and ironic. Now that Rufus himself had no place to go—*'cause my house fell down and I can't live here no mo',* sang Bessie—he heard the line and tone of the singer, and he wondered how others had moved beyond the emptiness and horror which faced him now.[18]

In the tale that Smith has woven Rufus hears a confirmation of his own broke-down condition. There is a deep sense of completion in Rufus' relationship to Smith's song, for he hears it as an apotheosis of his own experience, as a crystallization of his own feelings about his situation. Hearing his problem with no imagination of a solution, Rufus is completely inside his identification with the song, and is left to wonder how others have moved past such knowledge, past consciousness of a wholesaledly negative condition. It is important that Baldwin has chosen lyrics from two different points in the song, with the first speaking on the impact of catastrophe on black people in general—"There's thousands of people"—and the second naming the narrator's specific experience—"cause my house fell down." Baldwin's choice expresses the double nature of Rufus' condition, at once naming a specifically social burden, a burden structured by both the larger social workings of race and gender, and also naming Rufus' very specific experience of having been put out of doors: Rufus recognizes himself as part of a multitude, as having membership among the thousands of people who ain't got no place to go. The irony of that identification, however, is that such membership can never, technically, offer a home.

Spinning in the background, laying down the track for his coming demise, "Backwater Blues" speaks to Rufus in ways that his friend does not hear. For even as Smith's song sings to Rufus a confirmation of his own confrontation with "emptiness and horror," Vivaldo hears something else, interrupting Rufus' contemplation with a suggestion that he leave town, telling him that "Maybe it would be a good idea for you to make a change of scene, Rufus. Everything around here will just keep reminding you—sometimes it's better just to wipe the slate clean and take off." Where Rufus hears desolation, Vivaldo hears opportunity. The house is gone; this place is all fucked up; you might as well move on. But, for Rufus, the problem is not with what surrounds him; it is with something on the inside that cannot be left behind because it travels easy. As far as he can tell, people like himself are "on their ass out there, too."

With no clue as to how to recover from what he hears crystallized in Smith's blues, and without someone who might find similar resonance in Smith's song, Rufus' destruction is deepened. Here, together in Vivaldo's apartment, there is no milieu, only space, which Rufus tries desperately to close:

> "I wish I could tell you what it was like," Rufus said, after a long silence. "I wish I could undo it."
>
> "Well, you can't. So please start trying to forget it."

Rufus' statement draws equivalence between telling and undoing, which aligns this telling with confession. Telling cannot undo the past, but it does act on the future, which is unfortunately foreclosed by Vivaldo's refusal to hear the nuance in the equivalence, to hear Rufus' need. His "Well you can't" moves against both halves of Rufus' mirrored statement, as in the place of telling Vivaldo suggests forgetting. Perhaps accepting Rufus' telling would generate too much intimacy for Vivaldo—too much seeing, too much hearing, too much knowing. Weeks earlier, holding Leona as she wept in the wake of her final battle with Rufus, Vivaldo had come close to the edge of such an understanding, "A light was turning on inside him, a dreadful light. He saw—dimly—dangers, mysteries, chasms which he had never dreamed existed."[19] But the moment passes, not to return until his final confrontation with Ida, Rufus' younger sister whom Vivaldo takes as a lover after Rufus' death. Later, when he is desperate to understand this formerly refused knowledge—what "he had always known, but never dared to believe"—Ida finally gives it to him. But as soon as she begins to tell him her story, to let him in, he immediately comes to understand what is at stake in such knowing, for "She was not locking him out now; . . . rather he was being locked in."[20] The space closes, hot and tight.

Like Ida explaining to Vivaldo that the roots of their present relation go "too far back" to explain, Rufus cannot forget, and thus cannot choose not to know. He can remember, but he cannot tell because to tell would be to ask his friends to remember something they refuse to know about the present. This is evident in his relationship to Leona, whom Vivaldo correctly identifies as an "unwitting heiress of generations of bitterness." She does not know that, for Rufus, she is a site of memory, her skin, her hair, and her eyes constantly returning him to where he does not want to be but cannot help but go. His encounters with Leona offer him passage into an interior self that is itself tethered to a racial past—acts of remembrance that are about her, but that also have nothing to do with her at all, further ensnaring them in a relationship in which erotic sensation is inextricable from racial difference: staring at her throat on the night of their first encounter,

"He wanted to put his mouth there and nibble it slowly, leaving it black and blue."[21]

The language of this desire, written in bruises, also takes its vocabulary from Andy Razaf's "(What did I do to be so) Black and Blue?," which is probably best known as part of Louis Armstrong's repertoire.[22] In that song, Razaf's lyrics name sexual loneliness—"Cold, empty bed,/ Springs hard as lead,"—as an effect of racial discrimination—"Gentlemen prefer them light,/ Wish I could fade, can't make the grade," and in the process comes to what Robert O'Meally has called a "tragedy-haunted meditation on white racism," a song that names being black as an effect of racism, and having the blues as an effect of being black. Even when not marking the body with physical violence, racism's power is expressed in a language of suffering so deep that it arrives as a message written in stone, written on the body, an ancient curse:

> How sad I am, each day I feel worse,
> My mark of Ham seems to be a curse!
> How will it end? Ain't got a friend,
> My only sin, Is my skin.
> What did I do, to be so black and blue?[23]

Rufus' desire to make Leona black and blue is tied to his desire to know something about her—could she be made like him?—and also to his desire to make her know what it feels like to sin in skin, to never control the power and meaning of one's own social significations. For it is not that Leona's skin does not signify; whiteness is not some neutral transparent thing. The difference is in how much one must care about this signification, which Rufus must. Looking at her on the night of their first encounter, Rufus is prompted to memory:

> He remembered, suddenly, his days in boot camp in the South and felt again the shoe of a white officer against his mouth. He was in his white uniform, on the ground, against the red, dusty clay. Some of his colored buddies were holding him, were shouting in his ear, helping him to rise. The white officer, with a curse, had vanished, had gone forever beyond the reach of vengeance. His face was full of clay and tears and blood; he spat red blood into the red dust.[24]

In her skin Leona briefly transports Rufus back to the South, to a material encounter with a spectral whiteness, a manifestation of white power embodied in the vanishing Naval officer. The signifiers of the force of this encounter slip together, as the image of Rufus' face, clay, tears, and blood, is consolidated in the image of his red blood hitting the iconic Southern red dust. The officer, meanwhile, vanishes, but the trace of his power, his right to appear and disappear at will, remains. It is in Rufus' dirty and stained white uniform, in his tears that must go unredeemed in the absence of final battle. Leona, however, of course cannot see in herself what Rufus sees, and in this way Baldwin also reveals the destruction inherent in how Rufus has come into being through racism, as he attempts to use violence to make Leona know what he knows, to see what he sees; as he attempts to somehow grasp the spectral signification shifting behind her whiteness and to take back from it the possession of his own body. Alone together in their little apartment, with her screaming and his hitting, they generate a shared space of meaning, but one that comes without knowing and without sympathy. Their conflict might have origins in the symbolic, but it emerges as nothing but real, red clay, tears, and bruised flesh.

The depth of Rufus' attachment to the past in fact impacts every conflict Rufus has with his white friends in the present, and this difference continually plays out as a misunderstanding as to whether what enrages or harms Rufus comes from them or himself. Racism inhabits Rufus—it is in his experiences, in his past, in his understandings of the things that happen to people like him—but it is also in his white friends, who in their skin constantly remind him of unspoken pasts uneasily left behind:

> . . . to remember Leona was also—somehow—to remember the eyes of his mother, the rage of his father, the beauty of his sister. It was to remember the streets of Harlem, the boys on the stoops, the girls behind the stairs and on the rooftops, the white policeman who had taught him how to hate. . . .

In each encounter with Leona, memory moves across disjuncture as what is reminded to Rufus bespeaks a past that is itself about race, but also, somehow, not. Her but not her, him but not him: haunting. To remember Leona was

> to remember the beat: *A nigger*, said his father, *lives his whole life, lives and dies according to a beat. Shit, he humps to that beat and the baby he throws up in there, well, he jumps to it and comes out nine months later like a goddamn tambourine*. . . . The beat—in Harlem in the summertime one could almost see it, shaking above the pavements and the roof.[25]

The beat, simultaneously comforting and discomfiting in its temporal syncopation, haunts and tracks. It describes an encounter with the self that is also, somehow, outside of the self, "shaking above the pavements and the roof." Heat: "And he had fled, so he had thought, from the beat of Harlem, which was simply the beat of his own heart."

At the peak of his disagreement with Vivaldo, after Vivaldo has suggested that Rufus leave town, Baldwin gives us the following:

> "I guess you think," said Rufus, malevolently, "that it's time I started trying to be a new man."
>
> There was a silence. Then Vivaldo said, "It's not so much what I think. It's what you think."
>
> Rufus watched the tall, lean, clumsy white boy who was his best friend, and felt himself nearly strangling with the desire to hurt him.[26]

The same desire for violence would come to Rufus in similar moments with Leona. Indeed, as Vivaldo says this, Rufus remembers the violence with which he would respond to her. He remembers their fighting, him beating her, him raping and humiliating her, and that in all of this, every time, "one storm was like the other":

> "Rufus," Leona had said—time and time again—"ain't nothing wrong in being colored."

Rufus remembers how in these moments, he "simply looked at her coldly, from a great distance, as though he wondered what on earth she was trying to say. His look seemed to accuse her of ignorance and indifference."

The temporal difference between Rufus and his friends—which is to say the way in which he experiences his present as subject to the past—is also experienced by Rufus as a spatial distance. Completely alienated from his lover and his best friend, he literally experiences the moment as an alien, as foreign or unable to comprehend Leona's speaking, wondering "what on earth she was trying to say." As Rufus remembers these encounters, Vivaldo has already flipped *Backwater Blues,* and its B-side, Smith's "Empty Bed Blues," is the new tune to his thoughts. "My springs is getting rusty, sleeping single like I do," in strong resonance with Razaf's original lyrics to "Black and Blue," in which we hear of an "Old empty bed," with "Springs hard as lead."[27] In this way, the sexual drama is also reminded to us as a specifically racial drama as well.

The night Rufus first meets Leona, before they have sex on a balcony overlooking the Hudson, the same river where he will later commit suicide, Rufus imagines hearing "a faint murmur coming from the water." Tracking and unfolding the vague sensation, Rufus suddenly recalls the image of a dead child, being carried down his block after drowning in the Harlem River: "He had never forgotten the bend of the man's shoulders or the stunned angle of his head."[28] This image of a father, carrying the body of his dead son, resonates with a later story that comes in the aftermath of Rufus' own death, a story told to Vivaldo by Ida. It is the story of what happens to Rufus' body after he falls:

> My father stared at it . . . It didn't look like Rufus, it was—terrible—from the water, and he must have *struck* something going down, or in

> the water, because he was so broken and lumpy—and ugly. *My* brother. And my father stared at it—and he said, They don't leave a man much, do they? His own father was beaten to death with a hammer by a railroad guard. And they brought his father home like that.[29]

Standing on the bridge, with Billie Holiday's "All of Me" lamenting all the pieces of him that can never be returned to him—"You took the best/ Why not take the rest?"—Rufus' face is again covered with tears, "splashed with salt water." Leaning out and over the Hudson, a still-salty river known for changing its daily flow from south to north and back again, Rufus thinks in a language of pure and tragic identification: "It was cold and the water would be cold"; then, "He was black and the water was black."[30] *There's thousands of people, ain't got no place to go.* He jumps.

THE LOWLANDS

It is important to note that the novel's most problematic listening is that of Rufus himself, particularly as Baldwin's writing of Rufus' demise makes blues lyrics speak for his predicament, therefore leaving us to imagine that having the blues is somehow equivalent to listening to the blues, or even to blues music itself. But as Albert Murray insists in *Stomping the Blues*, there is an important difference between having the blues and what is performed by the music, for even as "The blues are synonymous with low spirits. Blues music is not."[31] The sacrifice offered up by a blues performer, on stage or on the record, is a front, as this revelation of an interior self left vulnerable in the wake of a blow plays an important and self-conscious role in a specifically social ritual of recognition and expiation. As Murray reminds us, even in the face of the most broken blues performance, the audience would be "normally expected to respond not with uneasiness and gestures of fear and trembling but with warm person-to-person intimacy that was both robust and delicate," responses that speak to a sense of the blues dancehall as also "a temple," a site of purification.[32] The sentiments expressed in blues lyrics might be flat on the ground, but such lyrics also elicit laughter at their most desolate, murmurs of agreement at their most naughty, and whooping and hollering at their most destitute—all proper responses to what Adam Gussow describes as "the blues' animating paradox, their curious compressed yoking of tragedy and comedy."[33] In the moment of sharing things that are otherwise unspeakable, the unspeakable in its distance from its origin becomes really *pathetic*—and might thus be better recognizable as such, as that which hurts can thus also come to be understood as really funny, or too absurd, or just pleasurable in the muddy wallow.

The simultaneous collapse and expansion of this distance is reminiscent of Paul de Man's description of allegory in "The Rhetoric of Temporality," which I mention in the previous chapter. In that chapter, de Man's commentary is useful towards understanding the painful interplay between identification and ignorance—remembering and never knowing—in Countee Cullen's poem, "Heritage." Here, however, we can see how the flips and slips endemic to blues performance might shed a different light on what is at stake in the difference between symbol and allegory. To quote again:

> Whereas the symbol postulates the possibility of an identity or identification, allegory designates primarily a distance in relation to its own origin, and, in renouncing the nostalgia and desire to coincide, it establishes a language in the void of this temporal difference. In so doing, it prevents itself from an illusory identification with the non-self, which is now fully, though painfully, recognized as a non-self.[34]

In the kind of aesthetic experience made available in the blues we find the B-side of de Man's claim, for what he describes as painful recognition might also be experienced as pleasurable. Fixing experience onto someone or somewhere else makes expiation possible, as the blues pulls folk in close but also pushes them away: it's just like you, but not you. Motivated by pain, but not the pain itself, the blues allegorize the common and terrible. As Angela Davis puts it, such songs transcend singular experience, coming to carry greater social signification as "the aesthetic distance achieved through music forges a consciousness that imagines community among the people who share glimpses of the possibility of eventually moving beyond this oppression."[35] And this distance is no cold thing, for it is a distance that enables a collapse between now and then, self and other. Transmitting memory and knowledge across discrete experiences, the blues is haunting, the music itself arising out of the gap between an event and its representation. If we follow Baldwin's sense that "The occurrence of an event is not the same thing as knowing what it is that one has lived through," then we might also imagine that coming into this knowledge makes space for recovery, no longer stunned by the hammer's blow.

A particularly interesting example comes in "Backwater Blues" itself. Written by Smith in 1926, "Backwater Blues" is sung from the perspective of a woman being evacuated from her home in a Mississippi River flood. It begins by setting the scene:

> When it rains five days and the skies turn dark as night
> When it rains five days and the skies turn dark as night
> Then trouble's takin' place in the lowlands at night[36]

Because they are situated in the conditional rather than in the past or present, the song's opening lines resonate with the mythical, as if spoken from a place of broad knowledge. "Trouble," further builds this mythos, explaining everything and nothing at the same time. (Rufus once tells Vivaldo, "If you can't see it, I can't tell you.")[37] It points in two directions, first to the literal troubles brought by the storm's waters, and then also to a sense of all the other kinds of native trouble that will be exacerbated by the event, the kind of trouble that already takes place "in the lowlands at night." That this trouble might be about more than the storm itself emerges in the girl's wondering on where she might go, which conveys a sense of her not only needing to get out of her house, but also needing to get away from this troubled place.

This is not surprising, for living in a backwater is, in its essence, *about* trouble. In everyday language, "backwater" designates a place understood as socially outside the mainstream or behind the times. But we must remember that backwaters, populated areas designated as so unimportant to the polity that they might be sacrificed in the event of a flood, are literally and figuratively kept outside and behind for a reason. Backwater living thus indicates a social condition of being subject to the dual tyrannies of the natural and social worlds. As Davis points out:

> The seasonal rains causing the Mississippi River to flood its banks are part of the unalterable course of nature, but the sufferings of untold numbers of black people who lived in towns and the countryside along the river also were attributable to racism. Black people were often considered expendable, and their communities were forced to take the overflow of backwaters in order to reduce the pressure on the levees. While most of the white people remained safe, black people suffered the wrath of the Mississippi, nature itself having been turned into a formidable weapon of racism.[38]

As I have argued elsewhere, there are ways in which the Mississippi's floodings and flows have been used as positive and generative metaphors for African American memory, for instance Toni Morrison's description of racial memory as the triumph of water returning to its natural course.[39] Yet despite the resonance of her metaphor, it is also important to remember that in its very materiality a flood is also a repetition of an enduring and terrible reality. Set below sea level, surrounded by the levee walls that hold back the temporarily tamed rivers and lakes, backwater residents live in the shadow of their own vulnerability, in the face of their own social death on the American scene.

"Backwater Blues" thus not only testifies to living without a certain kind of security, but also to living with the knowledge that one's own interests have been sacrificed to another's. It names a social condition, a condition resonant across discrete experiences of race, class, and gender. Once sung aloud, the phrase "backwater blues" collects an already extant social meaning, revealing a kind of knowingness far from Baldwin's assertion mentioned earlier in this chapter, that most people live in denial of the blows they have suffered. The event, the flood, prompts the emergence of an old thing, something already there and, in Toni Morrison's sense of rememory, "waiting for you":[40]

> Backwater blues done call me to pack my things and go
> Backwater blues done call me to pack my things and go
> Cause my house fell down and I can't live there no more

When Smith sings at the end of the song that the "Backwater blues done call me to pack my things and go," she is speaking to the haunting history of racism that has always and already made herself and people like her vulnerable to catastrophe. The singer, then, can be called *by* this blues, called *to* this blues.

In 1927, the year the song was released, Smith's invocation of being called by the backwater blues would have found easy recognition and reception with black audiences well aware of such events, especially since that year saw one of the most catastrophic episodes of Mississippi River flooding.[41] The prevalence of news about the event, then, might account for the matter-of-factness with which Smith sings the song's most catastrophic lines, "When it thunders and lightnin' and the wind begins to blow/ There's thousands of people ain't got no where to go."

Paradoxically, the musical rendition of the song's constituent desolation also works explicitly against the abyss it would otherwise name. If we return to Murray's sense that the blues performance is grounded in expiation, one could easily imagine the audience's response in stark counterpoint to the story's lyrics. I always imagine, for instance, that when Smith sings of the little boat coming to rescue her, laughter would come easily to her audience. The house is gone, your stuff is gone, and here *they* come, to row you away, coming too late to take you to no place in a boat that might not very well make it anyway. I mean, *really*. There is an authority in such moments of laughter, a power that comes with irony. The pain is not gone, but it has been fixed and tamed by a pleasurable tune, ripe for repeating over and over again.

Irony is written on the very surface of "Backwater Blues." After the rains have come and the floods have destroyed the lowlands, Smith has her own protagonist speak from a faraway place of displacement, singing:

> Then I went and stood upon some high old lonesome hill
> Then I went and stood upon some high old lonesome hill
> Then looked down on the house where I used to live

With total destruction at her feet, the woman's distance from the material event, the flood, allows her a certain omnipotence, a power of vision possessed in spite of an otherwise complete disenfranchisement. Like Rufus in the scene of his death, she is away and alone, she "upon some high old lonesome hill," he on the rail of the George Washington Bridge, high above the Hudson River. However, her capacity for speaking her pain, the storytelling that is the very precondition of the song, reveals an important difference from Rufus, despite the song's resonance with this personal experience. For where Smith gives us irony in the woman's literal and figurative distance from the event—the fact of the song's performance, which means the woman is not actually alone; the coolness with which she looks upon the devastation; and the sense of omnipotence conveyed by her situation high above that devastation—Baldwin instead gives us an identification with the event's symbolism, with its enduring meaning: "He was black and the water was black."[42]

Even as Baldwin's inclusion of the "Backwater Blues" puts Rufus' suffering in specifically collective terms, there is something eminently isolated and isolating in how Rufus' hears it. He fails to realize that even as the blues looks into the eye of "the emptiness and horror," there is indeed a beyond. But without an audience, without a community with whom to suffer this new insight Rufus cannot bear alone the reality he hears reflected in Smith's lyrics. There is no whooping, no hollering, no affirmation of anything outside of the song's haunting prophecy. There is no irony, no melody. There is only word—line—and tone. Rather than be called to community, Rufus is driven from his friend's home, and then later from his former jazz haunt. His movement away from comfort is critical because it is a symptom of how he has become eminently susceptible to the world's violence, how he has been shaken by the past's reverberations, now fully structuring the present. Instead of moving away from the backwater, away from the memories of the past and the simultaneously interior and exterior pain water signifies, he becomes it.

THE BEST

It is important, however, not to overstate Rufus' inability to come into the fold as specifically *his* failure, for by the time of his death the reader has likely come to see why Rufus is alone. As Melvin Dixon points out, Rufus, black, bisexual, and an avant-garde artist, is "forever outside the realm of redemption offered by the church or by society at large." Constrained by dominant and dominating notions of homestead, and attendant requirements of good, steady job and de facto heterosexuality—"Rufus," he once imagines his sister repeating, "Don't you know we're depending on you?"—men like Rufus "must come to different terms as best as they can with the spatial and spiritual dimensions sanctioned by church and society," which also means that "the need for alternate space, refuge, or shelter looms paramount."[43] In a final and direct contrast with the hot and sweaty milieu in which Rufus reaches his most sustaining identifications, the jazz club where he remembers himself performing at the novel's beginning, Rufus arrives at another club, a downtown place where, sitting with his white friends, he immediately feels "black, filthy, foolish."[44] This is where he starts to hear Smith's "Jailhouse Blues": "*I wouldn't mind being in jail but I've got to stay there so long . . . ,*" as being black and filthy and foolish is also made continuous in this scene with Rufus' sexual desire for men. Propelled away from Vivaldo, whose attention has been drawn to his ex-girlfriend Jane, Rufus knows there is a girl for him too, but he does not want her, instead escaping to the bathroom, which is soon revealed as a prison, as a holding cell for thousands of people who ain't got no place to go:

> It smelled of thousands of travelers, oceans of piss, tons of bile and vomit and shit. He added his stream to the ocean, holding that most despised part of himself loosely between two fingers of one hand. *But I've got to stay there so long. . . .* He looked at the horrible history splashed furiously on the walls—telephone numbers, cocks, breasts, balls, cunts, etched into these walls with hatred. *Suck my cock. I like to get whipped. I want a hot stiff prick up my ass. Down with the Jews. Kill the niggers. I suck cocks.*[45]

As a place of abjection, a place for that which has been cast off, the bathroom symbolizes and concretizes Rufus' marginal status. In his description of this place, Baldwin draws an equivalence between expressing racial hatred and experiencing non-normative sexual desire, making both violence against others and foreclosed desire between the self and others part and parcel of the same shame. In this way the bathroom is not quite the space of the cast off; it is the space of evacuation, a space for bodies for whom expiation has devolved into expurgation, into experiences of selves made unfamiliar and horrible in this signification of self-violence. As the water leaves his body, Rufus can barely stand the touch of his own body, "holding that most despised part of himself loosely between two fingers of one hand." Before he leaves the club, abandoning his friends, he washes his hands "very carefully," dries them on "the filthy roller towel," and heads for the subway. Approaching the stairs, he suddenly remembers his mother's hand, which brings a long-ago feeling of safety, coming from far away. But in the present, shamed and hands dirty, he can only imagine death and destruction as he descends the stairs, to hit the A train that will take him home.

As the train barrels north to Harlem, Rufus sees a girl who reminds him of his sister Ida. She moves to sit as far away from him as possible. Baldwin then gives us the following:

> . . . [the train] came into the bright lights of 125 Street. The train gasped and moaned to a halt. *He had thought he would get off here*, but he watched the doors open, watched them leave. It was mainly black people who left. *He had thought that he would get off here* and go home; but he watched the girl who reminded him of his sister as she moved sullenly past white people and stood for a moment on the

> platform before walking toward the steps. Suddenly he knew that he was never going home any more. (my emphasis)

We know that Ida adores her older brother, but in this girl's denial Rufus is shamed—black, filthy, foolish. Perhaps he thinks that he has failed Ida, a failure that can be read in terms of race, but also in terms of sex and gender, insofar as both his sexual relationship with a white woman and his disavowed bisexuality constitute betrayals of the black middle class domestic aspiration of which he is ostensibly the dream. We can also see this in Baldwin's use of repetition in this pivotal passage. As the only other instance of such repetition in *Another Country*, it formally resonates with the saxophonist's solo. On first rendition, "He had thought he would get off here" is juxtaposed with the reminder that the train has arrived in Harlem's heart, with "mainly black people" leaving the train at 125th Street. On second rendition, "He had thought he would get off here" is set against the departure of the girl, moving "sullenly" through the sea of whites, hesitating on the platform. A flash comes to Rufus in the interval of that hesitation, as he realizes he can never go home. Is it her sullenness? Her loneliness? In his imagining that his sex is his best thing, that only his heterosexual domestication could help her in her struggle, Rufus can only see failure: "You took the best/ So why not take the rest?"

Away and alone, Rufus' encounter with the backwater blues is complete and unmitigated, as he suffers for himself and his meaning, for his personal desires and for the enslavement of those desires to a particular history and its future meanings. Hearing the song's call and not its signal—identifying with its origin, water and the abyss, rather than with its purpose, memorialization and recovery—Rufus answers: he packs his shit and goes.

> The bridge was nearly over his head, intolerably high; but he did not see the water. He felt it, he smelled it. He thought how he had never before understood how an animal could smell water. But it was over there. . . .
>
> He was black and the water was black.[46]

If we return to the earlier scene of the saxophonist playing, we can see that even though they are trying to seem cool and detached, Rufus and his bandmates sweat when the saxophonist blows because they are working *hard* to create and maintain the aesthetic distance necessary to the transformation of the soloist's blow from a mere retelling of the event of the blow into the haunting and affecting transmission of a newly received prior knowledge of the blow's impact. When listening to "Backwater Blues," one can hear the piano that Baldwin describes as "stoic, and ironic" bearing witness to the singer's loss, matching every turn in the narrative with apt illustration and more than a touch of humor, commenting on every fucked up thing with loving and empathic riffs, surviving. For Rufus, though, the magic of such understanding has passed away from him, and all that's left is the question, over and over again: *do you love me?* At his funeral, we sing in a gospel retroactively tinged by the blues:

> I'm a stranger, don't drive me away.
> I'm a stranger, don't drive me away.
> If you drive me away, you may need me some day,
> I'm a stranger, don't drive me away.[47]

3 Behind Carma and Rosie

Come, brother, come. Let's lift it;
Come now, hewit! roll away!
Shackles fall upon the Judgment Day
But lets not wait for it.

God's body's got a soul,
Bodies like to roll the soul,
Cant blame God if we dont roll
Come, brother, roll, roll![1]

—Jean Toomer, "Cotton Song"

I don't mind bein' in jail, but I got to stay there so long, so long
I don't mind bein' in jail, but I got to stay there so long, so long
When every friend I have is done shook hands and gone

You better stop your man from tickling me under my chin, under my chin,
You better stop your man from tickling me under my chin, under my chin,
'Cause if he keeps on tickling, I'm sure gonna take him on in.[2]

—Bessie Smith, "Jailhouse Blues"

In *Another Country*, Rufus' time at the crossroads between trying to live and choosing to die is thematized in a series of songs sung by Bessie Smith and Billie Holiday. "Jailhouse Blues," for instance, echoes Rufus' racial and sexual alienation as he watches his best friend and unrequited lover Vivaldo's attention move from him to his on-again off-again girlfriend, Jane.[3] By this point in *Another Country*, Baldwin has already constituted Vivaldo as doubly unattainable for Rufus, as his whiteness limits his usefulness as Rufus' friend and his straightness forecloses him as an appropriate object of desire. Indeed, even as everyone in *Another Country* is at any moment kept from what he or she wants, competing and complicit social restrictions on interraciality and homosexuality lock tight the door to his desires, shaming Rufus for ever wanting anything at all. As Rufus sees it, it's not the being in this lonely jail that is the problem; it is the complete *inevitability* of his fall from grace that rocks him, as his white friends dismiss the racial specificity of his predicament and his body continuously rebels against the self-avowed heterosexuality that in *Another Country* is exposed as a false signifier for black male identity.

As one of several songs soundtracking the first section of Baldwin's novel, Smith's "Jailhouse Blues" names some haunting convergences between our interior selves and our social selves, between the needs of the flesh and the symbolic registers through which we express and therefore come to know those selfsame needs. In Smith's song, this convergence between the body that is controlled and the body that will take control is symbolized in her figure of the jail, in the tension between the plea, "Look here, Mr. Jailkeeper, put another girl in my stall," and the threat, "Cause if he keeps on tickling, I'm sure gonna take him in." Through Smith's jailhouse we are made to see how each emerges out of the other, and are also offered insight into why Rufus' death resonates so well in *Another Country*. Each of the novel's characters has had his or her own taste of racial or sexual incarceration, and in the wake of Rufus' death each has come in various degrees to know that the key to freedom is only available in one's own care for the self, even when that self seems most distant, most unlovable, and most locked away, another country. The irony of course is that this care for the self is best demonstrated through one's love for another, in a care for bodies that transcends difference. In Smith's song, as in *Another Country*, being unable to touch others is the same as being jailed.

Smith's song also, however, lays out the terms for resistance, which comes in the small flirtation, the tickle under the chin. The tickle is significant because it is so small. It is an anticipation, a reminder. In this way, Smith's song picks up some of the sound and signification of the old black work songs out of which Smith's signature genre grew. There may be shackles, and her back may be to the wall, but that tickle surely tickles. As we are reminded in Jean Toomer's "Cotton Song," *God's body's got a soul,/ Bodies like to roll the soul,/ Cant blame God if we dont roll/ Come, brother, roll, roll!*

Evocative of field calls, here shouted out between men, "Cotton Song" is a poem that appears in the first section of Jean Toomer's 1919 modernist masterpiece, *Cane*, which is itself a montage of prose, poetry, and music, as well as a concluding dramatic piece.[4] The prose pieces in *Cane*'s first section are mainly contemplative, characterized by long moments of looking at women and narrated by an anonymous man. In the slow sweep of the text's first section, the vivacity of the worker's singing—"roll, roll!"—plays as particularly visceral, breaking the poem's sound and spirit away from the mournful gazing characteristic of the section's other pieces. Whereas "Cotton Song" sings that "Bodies like to roll the soul," in Toomer's other texts it seems that bodies—which are often those of women—are at best present in the text simply to roll the souls of men. Mainly presented as objects of a distant narrator's gaze, these bodies—female, black, and Southern—seldom speak and barely move, always invoked in the name of something else, bespeaking memory, loss, race. Much as Baldwin sacrifices Rufus so that others might learn to live, Toomer sacrifices women so that the South can find allegorical representation in the gap between what is and isn't, between reality and that which we know thereas. As Nathaniel Mackey has written, it is by virtue of his sacrificed women that Toomer's writing in *Cane* "is haunted throughout by a ghost of aborted splendor, a specter written into its much-noted lament for the condition of the women it portrays—woman as anima, problematic 'parting soul.'"[5] Women are displaced from their bodies so that those bodies might carry Toomer's meaning, like Karintha, carrying beauty.[6] It is not that Karintha is not beautiful, but to describe her as carrying beauty draws attention to the gap between that beauty as hers and that beauty as something to be apprehended in relation to her.

ASHÉ

To get a sense of how women's bodies haunt the very possibility for meaning in *Cane*, turn to "Carma," a two page tale in which Toomer foregrounds a narrative movement between sight, smell, and sound in order to shift the reader between different times and spaces. By doing so Toomer avoids conventional narrative recollection, instead generating a generative experience of reading that trumps the space and time of linear narrative. By keeping *Cane* firmly in the present, Toomer is able to present the South, rather than merely representing it, thus allowing *Cane* to stand in as a best possible expression of that past, as a place kept alive in the moment of reading. Rather than attempt to capture a waning milieu by monumentalizing it, by freezing and encapsulating it, Toomer instead asks the reader to experience the text's narrative moments as they pass across the page.[7] In "Carma," this plays out as a gerund experience consolidated both in the heavy repetition that characterizes the story and in its narrative emphasis on the kinds of contemporaneously unaligned sensations that in retrospect come together to create any present: smell, touch, sweat, and sound, each in hindsight able to invoke the totality of the others. The past comes as a cipher, for karma is always about return, about how every present is doomed to reappear in the future, a future that can thus only be constituted in relation to the past, a past that has never become a proper past in the Western sense of being *gone*.

"Carma" begins with the narrator watching Carma drive a mule down the road, a sight he summarizes as "Nigger woman driving a Georgia chariot down an old dust road."[8] Humorous on its surface—that surely is no chariot—the narrator's ironic description also foreshadows Carma's allegorical status in the text. Watched hard by the narrator, she eventually "disappears in a cloudy rumble at some indefinite point along the road." But as her body falls gently out of the text, something else comes into being in her place, in lieu of that which is symbolized in her body. What arrives is a continuation of the narrator's first epiphany: looking into her "mangrove gloomed face," he suddenly realizes that "God has left the Moses-people for the nigger"—for a people whom the narrator now suddenly comprehends as a chosen and therefore timeless people. To be chosen is to be timeless, as to be so keeps the future of a people beyond the grasp of the present and therefore outside the space of exigency, held there by the promise of promise. She is the covenant, a site of memory in whom is collected the meaning of prior and future worlds.

Indeed, carried away from himself in his meditation on Carma, the narrator is brought into a simultaneously old and new present, into a ghostly environment of memory.[9] In his contemplation of the eternal, for which Toomer has made Carma a metonym, the narrator is displaced. The story's prose suddenly shifts, cuts to scene, switching into a redolent and sensuous environmental language:

> (The sun is hammered to a band of gold. Pine needles, like mazda, are brilliantly aglow. No rain has come to take the rustle from the falling sweet-gum leaves. Over in the forest, across the swamp, a sawmill blows its closing whistle. Smoke curls up. Marvelous web spun by the spider sawdust pile. Curls up and spreads itself pine-high above the branch, a single silver band along the eastern valley. A black boy . . . you are the most sleepiest man I ever seed, Sleeping Beauty . . . cradled on a gray mule, guided by the hollow sound of cowbells, heads for them through a rusty cotton field. From down the railroad track, the chug-chug of a gas engine announces that the repair gang is coming home. A girl in the yard of a whitewashed shack not much larger than the stack of worn tie piled before, sings. Her voice is loud. Echoes, like rain, sweep the valley. Dusk takes the polish from the rails. Lights twinkle in scattered houses. From far away, a sad strong song. Pungent and composite, the smell of farmyards is the fragrance of the woman. She does not sing; her body is a song. She is the forest, dancing. Torches flare . . . juju men, greegree, witch doctors . . . torches go out . . . The Dixie Pike has grown from a goat path in Africa.
>
> *Night.*
>
> Foxie, the bitch, slicks back her ears and barks at the rising moon.)[10]

Between Carma's disappearance on the road and the narrator's second telling of her tale comes the above scene, which is in form closer to a stage or script direction than to a prose description. Cinematic, it splits the story into its two halves, setting the scene for the narrator's retelling of Carma's "crudest melodrama" by interrupting the narrative with his own present. Whenever one tells a story, that telling is, by virtue of its being told and not experienced, always posterior to the moment being described.[11] The only present is the enunciative act, an event that is never *the* event, and which in its effect is generally understood as quite different from a dramatic performance, during which the audience is invited to imagine itself as participating in the unfolding moment, as experiencing the moment in its present.[12] Here, Toomer seizes upon the temporal and uses it to place the reader in the reading-moment in a way that assures that the reader will not only understand the milieu of Carma's tale, but will also have one foot in the milieu of its comprehension, the moment when the narrator remembers it. What matters most here, then, is the moment of comprehension, the aesthetic experience *qua* empathic knowing: insight.

This immersion in the present's presence, in the "pungent and composite" nature of its sights and sounds and smells, opens up a twilight space into which other memories can enter, but not as memory in the temporal sense—as an experienced past—but as memory in a spatial sense, as a memory of place and all that the *idea* of place contains. "The Dixie Pike has grown from a goat path in Africa"; thus is intimated as an unveiling in the present the gist of a heretofore assumedly-lost past. Insight comes as the "sad strong song" from "far away," a memory-sensation of a lost history. Night falls, and Foxie the bitch, the only female character in *Cane* who breaks-not-makes spells, barks, signaling the end of twilight, memory's space. "Carma," like all memory-texts, follows a logic of temporal conservation—nothing is ever lost. Like Cullen with his jungle cat and Hughes with his huts, Toomer only has the most vague and general language for what the narrator sees, juju, greegree, torches. Maybe, later, he would recover new words, new calls into this other world that is also the world: *axe, axé, ashé*.

"STICK TO THE PROMISE"

Because she is so much at the center of the story, it is easy to forget that Carma is not the subject of the story. She is, rather, the prompt to the narrator's storytelling, the crystallization of an insight that leads him to tell the story that makes up the second half of "Carma," the part that comes after the parenthetical. It is unclear whether this second part of the tale is told in order to explicate the insight the narrator comes to in the first, or if it is in fact the other way around. Regardless, there is a sense that only her tale, "the crudest melodrama," could have led him to look for or move toward that insight. And we must wonder, *why Carma*? Why is this exemplary text of shifting time and space also a small and domestic tale of a man out of town at work and his cheating wife? And why so much emphasis on her rights as a cheating wife: "Should she not take others, this Carma, strong as a man, whose tale as I have told it is the crudest melodrama?"[13]

Melodrama is tragedy on the local level, a moment of loss made more human and terrible by its orientation towards an audience. If "tragedy" broadly aspires to the universal, playing out as a humanist crisis of loss, struggle, and fate, melodrama aspires to the local: it is played out on the front porch. Keeping in mind that Toomer wrote *Cane* in a time of transition, at the cusp of the Great Migration, *Cane* must thus be understood as being produced in a moment of crisis. In "Carma," this anxiety around departure and its attendant instabilities is thematized as a crisis in heterosexual relation, as Carma's decision to take others brings to fruition the anxiety of male migrant workers. "Pungent and composite, the smell of farmyards is the fragrance of the woman." Elusive yet tangible, "fragrance" more than smell names that which reminds. It is the scent a woman leaves in her wake; not her essence, nor her, but rather that which crystallizes for the bystander the hopes and dreams of his future—as such dreams come into being through a memory of her: this home being remembered is not a place heretofore known. It is an idea about the future, a promise signified in "having" a woman. *Pungent and composite, the smell of farmyards is the fragrance of the woman.* The fragrance is the ghost, the displaced or misplaced signifier, a promise lost misrecognized as the promise itself.

I am reminded here of old work songs, in which women are figured as home and homestead, comfort and possession—but a home that might sashay away, or a homestead that may be taken over by another. Consider a version of the old work song "Rosie." Known to some as the "queen of Parchman Farm," "Rosie" was a much sung cipher in early to mid twentieth-century work songs.[14] The song is a call and response text, and the rhythm of that interaction, itself railed by the work, is central to hearing the song. The song leader, the leader of this particular gang goes by the name of C.B., sets his calls to the blow of the inmates' hammers, immediately preceding their response (typeset here in italics).[15] The response is then immediately followed with another blow, setting the stage for the return of the call. This particular rendition of the song begins with a statement that is both assertive and vaguely conditional:

Be my woman, gal, I'll
be your man.
Be my woman, gal, I'll
be your man

In this song, the very idea of woman only really comes into view as a relation: be my woman, *so that I may be* your man. This is a delicate balance, more gamble than assertion, for incarceration has concretized the distance between the two bodies of this relation, has in fact removed the men from the world in which their masculinity was consecrated, thus making more than enough space for a profound troubling. In the song, this trouble comes to us in the image of Rosie's behind, moving away from the men, who are left to themselves, singing on the line:

When she walks she rocks and
rolls be-hind
Ain't that enough to worry
a man's mind?

Here, Rosie's behind is a site of investment, drawing gazes to her. A site of memory, its rockin' and rollin' crystallizes that which they no longer have, in the place of which there can only be anxiety as its call may not be for them alone. Looking back, we might even think here of the sensuality with which the narrator describes his first sight of Carma, moving on down the road away from him, him watching her as she "stands behind the old brown mule,"

> driving the wagon home. It bumps, and groans, and shakes as it crosses the railroad track. She, riding it easy.

It is easy for her, but more for him. Clearly, she rolls his soul. For him this rolling makes possible a transcendence: he, watching her hard—so hard that she dematerializes into an idea of what it would mean to be fully in her.

In "Rosie," however, the men are far and away, trying to overcome their trouble with the word and thus introducing an interdiction in the center of the song:[16]

> Stick to the promise girl that
> *you made me.*
> Stick to the promise girl that
> *you made me.*
> Not gonna marry til
> *I go free.*

The promise, the word, is timeless because it is beyond the reach of the present, outside the space of exigency—even as the song's conflicting anxieties are underscored by its deep-throated melancholy, embodied in the passionate and on-the-verge-of-wordlessness of its refrain:

> Well, Rosie!
> *Aw lawd, gal.*
> Well, Rosie!
> *Aw lawd, gal.*

Everything and nothing is in that "Aw lawd gal." It is the sound of worry, but also strangely brave. Cool and detached when spoken from behind, "Aw lawd, gal" is as easily an exclamation of appreciation for the rock and roll as it is a lament for the fact that that the behind has, likely, rocked and rolled away.

CARMA IN THE BRAKE

If Rosie is a dream, an idea of a woman whose desires are controlled by the word, magical through and despite the hammer's blow, Carma, dressed "in overalls and strong as any man," is the truth. Carma was not the woman her husband Bane, working "away most of the time," needed her to be or become in his absence. But he was gone until when? and she was a woman, dressed "in overalls and strong as any man." In her strength and sexuality, Carma is beyond her present's gender assumptions and therefore outside the space of domestic exigency. When she breaks the promise—would she have ever even made such a promise?—when she breaks the promise she shatters the illusion that Bane's work away from home, be it migrant or gang, does not risk an irrecoverable loss, a loss that bears a striking and painful resemblance to slavery's domestic and sexual ruptures.[17] By choosing living over waiting, she shakes her husband's faith in ownership. If she is not his woman, is he a man?

Enraged by the stories of her infidelity, Bane chases her into a canebrake. She has a gun, and, insofar as the historical overdetermination that has built black womanhood into the locus of black masculinity is itself based in slavery—which as an institution is represented in Toomer's novel *as* cane—one could imagine that, having broken the promise perceived as the foundation to home, one could of course imagine that Carma would kill herself in the canefield. For if history can make demands on the future, then one could imagine that at this juncture it must demand her life. Much as Rufus sacrifices himself to an inability to fulfill a meaning put upon him by the social, so must she also, in her infidelity, be sacrificed to the promise itself. She must be given up to an idea that one can make the future different from the past, even if only by virtue of a limited possibility, by control over a small and personal domain, the bed and the home.

But that is not what happens, for "time and space have no meaning in a canefield." When the men bring Carma, presumed injured, back into the house:

> They placed her on the sofa. . . . Her eyes were weak and pitiable for so strong a woman. Slowly, then like a flash, Bane came to know that the shot she fired, with averted head, was aimed to whistle like a dying hornet through the cane. Twice deceived, and one deception proved the other.[18]

The men cannot find the wound, the site that would prove the sacrifice made and enable the re-articulation of the homestead. With such a wound she would die or be forgiven—another kind of death for a woman strong as any man. But, rather than sacrifice his heroine, Toomer, quite surprisingly, has her save herself, the antithesis of sacrifice. When the men cannot find the wound, Bane, whose role as husband is to officiate over this terrible sacrifice to the future of the homestead, realizes that Carma will not be recalled into this story, and in the repetition of refusal she thus proves herself as capable of the same refusal to cooperate that got her in trouble in the first place. This realization comes to Bane as an epiphany, which mirrors the flash of insight the narrator has when he first looks into Carma's face. Thus Bane's otherwise cryptic realization, that "one deception proved the other." When she chooses living over waiting, Carma shatters the illusion that migrant work—a kind of work that pulls disenfranchised men away from home—would not destroy heterosexual domesticity. "Pungent and composite, the smell of farmyards is the fragrance of the woman": Overdetermined, the smell of farmyards signals sustenance and possibility. Men in *Cane* smell this in women's wakes, this thing that lingers after she has gone or after you have left her, as wakes come after death.

A final example: In *Another Country*, Rufus remembers looking at his sister Ida, whose destiny it is to become a blues singer. She is standing by the window, wrapped in a beautiful shawl he has brought back from India.

> On the day that he gave it to her and she tried it on, something shook in him which had never been touched before. He had never seen the beauty of black people before. But, staring at Ida, who stood before the window of the Harlem kitchen, seeing that she was no longer merely his younger sister but a girl who would soon be a woman, she became associated with the colors of the shawl, the colors of the sun, and with a splendor incalculably older than the gray stone of the island on which they had been born. He thought that perhaps this splendor would come into the world again some day, into the world they knew.

Touched by the meaning of what he sees in her, Rufus comes unto a flash of insight:

> Ages and ages ago, Ida had not merely been the descendent of slaves. Watching her dark face in the sunlight, softened and shadowed by the glorious shawl, it could be seen that she had once been a monarch. Then he looked out of the window, at the air shaft, and thought of the whores on Seventh Avenue. He thought of the white police-men and the money they made on black flesh, the money the whole world made.[19]

At first glance, Rufus' response to Ida might be read in terms similar to the transportation experienced by Toomer's narrator, as he watches Carma going on down the road. But here, in what Rufus sees, there is nothing slippery, no interruption of the past on the present, no path to Africa. Almost, but not quite, for in Rufus' vision, the future, which emerges out of the past, is instead interrupted by the present. There is not even a view from the window, because this window only opens to a dark and trapped interior. Yet, for a brief moment, Rufus sees the sun in Ida's face, sees an emanation of something beautiful and recuperative, a light unlikely coming from a tenement airshaft in Harlem. One screen becomes another; Ida, a site of memory, a citation of *home* whose promised security is nostalgically constructed in retrospect: the idea of safety and return to what came before the

Middle Passage, the *sotto voce* of black American experience. The blues is karmic, and, as with many of slavery's hauntings, the truth of its losses is ciphered, beautiful and terrible:

> These *lieu de mémoire* are fundamentally remains . . . *lieu de mémoire*—moments of history, then returned; no longer quite life, not yet death, like shells on the shore when the sea of living memory has receded.[20]

"The Dixie Pike has grown from a goat path in Africa." *There's thousands of people ain't got no place to go.* The "sea of living memory" approaches in calls and recedes in blows. It could be seen that she had once been a monarch.

> Well, Rosie!
> *Aw lawd, gal*

4 Folded Sorrows in Kaufman and Toomer

> And, finally, need I add that I who speak here am bone of the bone and flesh of the flesh of them that live within the Veil?[1]
>
> —W.E.B. Du Bois, *The Souls of Black Folk*

> But when from a long-distant past nothing subsists, after the people are dead, after the things are broken and scattered, tastes and smell alone, more persistent, more faithful, remain poised a long time, like souls, remembering, waiting, hoping, amid the ruins of all the rest, and bear unflinchingly, in the tiny and almost impalpable drop of their essence, the vast structure of recollection.[2]
>
> —Marcel Proust, *Swann's Way*

In the passage above, Marcel Proust offers a narrative for how the past turns both into us and away from us. For even as one's contemplation of the past might be experienced as a return, this return can also be experienced as something foreign or apart from the self, as if belonging to a person who lived far away and long ago. As we have seen in previous chapters, this distance between the past as a personal event and its future status as foreign to the self is ripe and difficult, with implications both personal and political. Temporal distance, the difference between now and then, is important to one's sense of growth and change, as through remembrance meaning emerges as a narrative of events and their impact. At the same time, the memory through which such self-making is accomplished also has a life of its own, independent of the person who might otherwise be imagined as its owner, as the one singular to the particular experience of the event through which that memory came into being. We can hear this in the way Proust posits memory as surviving beyond the time of its origin, "waiting, hoping, amid the ruins of all the rest." Much like Toni Morrison's notion of rememory in *Beloved*, Proust speaks to how we are constituted by events whose meanings extend beyond our individual pasts and the futures thereof, by things that will always *be*, will always "be there for you, waiting for you," as Morrison puts it.[3]

Looked at too closely, there is something disconcerting in this distance and difference, because it puts our memory in excess of ourselves, never to disappear even as we will. And although in this project haunting has not been talked about as supernatural, there *is* something distinctly creepy about it. Departed but not gone; "remembering, waiting, hoping" in the spaces between our renditions of ourselves. Us but not us, ours but not ours, in their new unfamiliarity such memories have the power to haunt because they have been set loose from ownership. Haunting splits memory off from recall, yet these memories nevertheless come to us as familiar because they consolidate prior intuition, now transformed into something stable and whole that can itself be disseminated. In this way haunting offers an unexpected narrative for both interior and exterior experiences.[4]

In *Swann's Way*, the narrator's encounter with the madeleine offers a striking example of how bare acts of recollection might be experienced as unfoldings, not back into time but into the self, a self perhaps aware of loss, but not that something has actually been *lost*. The episode is worth recounting; for even though it provides an oft-cited *mise-en-scène* for remembrance and recovery, especially involuntary memory, it is also particularly interesting in its description of the initially alien nature of that arrival:

> Mechanically, dispirited after a dreary day with the prospect of a depressing morrow, I raised to my lips a spoonful of the tea in which I had soaked a morsel of the cake. No sooner had the warm liquid mixed with the crumbs touched my palate than a shiver ran through me and I stopped, intent upon the extraordinary thing that was happening to me. An exquisite pleasure had invaded my sense, something isolated, detached, with no suggestion of its origin. . . . I sensed that it was connected with the taste of the tea and the cake, but that it infinitely transcended those savours, could not, indeed, be of the same nature.[5]

By bringing him into an attendance of the sensate world, the shimmer of remembrance shakes him from the dullness of his day. The idea that it invades, "isolated" and "detached," describes the distance between the meaning "it"—a referent without clear reference—used to hold, and its new unfamiliarity in the present. Because of the uninvited nature of this arrival, bridging this difference between the felt and the known requires consciousness if it is to move from mere sense and into meaning; otherwise the sensation only repeats itself, each time diminished in the empty repetition.[6] Soon it comes to him, for his meditation is the drop of water that gives the sensation, the waking trace of what had lay dormant within him for years, the "colour and distinctive shape" that would make "it" something more than mere affect.

At the moment of recollection Proust's narrator feels pull taut string that tethers an ostensibly progressive arrow of time to a simultaneously absent and present origin: this thing that has come to him from the outside is in fact located within himself. Within every present moment is a parcel, folded and bearing, unflinchingly, all the threats that come with time's passage, threats of forgetting and of passing away. Like "little pieces of paper which until then are without character or form, but, the moment they become wet, stretch and twist and take on colour and distinctive shape, become flowers or houses or people, solid and recognizable," the narrator experiences time's refusal to really pass into goneness.[7] Nothing is ever lost; there are only absences of water.

FOLDED SORROWS

Whereas in *Swann's Way* the unfolding of the past is experienced as a bountiful revelation, in "I Have Folded My Sorrows" the Beat poet Bob Kaufman also speaks to moving past bare acts of remembering, but instead focuses on the weariness that might accompany unfolding and unpacking the accumulation of long years. Much like Proust's narrator, alone in his old room, Kaufman's narrator speaks a language that is at once huge and personal and quiet:

> I have folded my sorrows into the mantle of summer night,
> Assigning each brief storm its allotted space in time,
> Quietly pursuing catastrophic histories buried in my eyes.[8]

Kaufman's poem begins with a soft reckoning. There is control in the speaker's evocation of pain made manageable through acts of recollection, returned to consciousness so that they may be sifted and sorted and folded back again, caught so that they might finally be put away. As Wordsworth notes in "Essays Upon Epitaphs," a "smooth surface and so fair an outside" often hides profound agitation beneath its calm surface.[9] And indeed, the peace radiating from Kaufman's poem is on second look quite suspicious, for even as his speaker's careful strategy of approach and assignation seems so sensible, the description of this work as an encounter with "catastrophic histories" undermines his otherwise cool stance. Retrospection does not bring shock or horror, outrage or tears; the speaker's experience of memory instead registers as a kind of weariness in the absence of solutions to the past's pains, which are the selfsame pains through which the speaker's identity has been constituted. The memories are his, buried behind *his* eyes, even as "buried" suggests eyes that are closed, slow to reach consciousness.

Between the diminishment of agency and the invocation of catastrophe, we cannot help but wonder if these memories might have been buried for a reason. Indeed, soon after this encounter the poem's speaker lists a series of facts. It is unclear whether they are admissions or revelations:

> And yes, the world is not some unplayed Cosmic Game,
> And the sun is still ninety-three million miles from me,
> And in the imaginary forest, the shingled hippo becomes
> the gay unicorn.
>
> (4–7)

Neither theology nor science offers a knowledge that can abate this weariness, as the poet sees himself as having no more access to the kind of comfort each could offer than he would to the kinds of salvific transformations available in a fantasy world in which even the most abject are magically transformed. The speaker's iteration also foregrounds the place of the reader in relation to these facts, as the reader appears in the poem as a silent interlocutor to whom his gently sardonic "yes" is addressed. *Thank you*, he seems to be saying, *for reminding me of the following*. If the blues might be understood in the ironic vein of laughing to keep from crying, in Kaufman's poem the sardonic introduces us to the notion of living to keep from dying, as having shingles marks the emergence of a latent illness, a pain thought already resolved, thought cured and gone away.

Address soon emerges again in the poem, as the speaker's anticipatory "no" makes clear to the reader that he or she should not apprehend his weariness as brooding or melancholy, not misrecognize it as a predictable symptom of an unhealthy fixation on the past—a criticism often levied against African Americans, who are continually brought to task for speaking of that which might supposedly heal if it could only be forgotten:

> No, my traffic is not addled keepers of yesterday's
> disasters,
> Seekers of manifest disembowelment on shafts of yesterday's
> pains.
>
> (8–11)

Here, "traffic" could be read as referencing a moral stance, *I do not traffic in lies*, or as referencing something in motion, trafficking through him—you might think here of the speaker in Countee Cullen's "Heritage": "Dear distress, and joy allied/ Is my somber flesh and skin,/ With the dark blood dammed within/ Like great pulsing tides of wine/ That, I fear, must burst the fine/ Channels of the chafing net/ Where they surge and foam and fret."[10] In Cullen's poem, the conflict between the self in its individuality and the self as beholden to a lost racial past produces a hot and rolling turmoil, ambivalence played out as a wet rebellion of body against mind. In Kaufman's poem, however, the turmoil insinuated by the word "traffic" is problematized by the word's possible signification in the opposite direction, for any signification of the word's moral sense diminishes the rise of that ambivalence onto the poem's surface. "My traffic is not"—*I shall not be moved*—the stability of his position sets him in clear opposition to the "addled keepers," they who would destroy themselves, evacuating meaning from their own lives in self-sacrifice to the past. Yet despite the clarity of his narration of who he is not, the poem's next line disrupts the assertion:

> Blues come dressed like introspective echoes of a journey.
>
> (12)

Kaufman's invocation of the blues reminds his reader that the speaker's balanced relationship to the past will not necessarily protect him from it. Here, the blues come from elsewhere, simultaneously other but also dressed in its resonance with the self.

Melancholy, the appearance of the blues breaks the poem, and even though the poet afterwards returns to the imagery with which the poem began, something has changed with the blues' ghostly arrival. Or maybe it is the case that things are the same, but must now be talked about a little bit differently by virtue of that arrival:

> And yes, I have searched the rooms of the moon on cold
> summer nights.
> And yes, I have refought those unfinished encounters.
> Still, they remain unfinished.
> And yes, I have at times wished myself something different.
>
> (14–17)

The poem's final lines echo its opening, each line displaying just enough internal difference that each moment named comes to highlight the arduousness of this poet's task. In these lines, the folding has become a searching; the night, though summer, is cold, not warm. Each act of assignation is a battle fought, but also an encounter unfinished—the catastrophes are complete, for it is only a wish that the poet's life could transform, could *be* different from that which has made the poet into a poet. Further, the fact of his address, the fact that the stabilization of his speaking self—his assertion—must come in response to an absent other reflects the extent to which that assertion has a home in the self, insofar as the question in fact literally comes from the self. The speaker's yessing and no-ing is anticipatory in the truest sense: he know the answers because it is he who is asking the questions. Here, then, is ambivalence, but it is masked as a response to another.

The very possibility for the poem is itself tied up with the catastrophes that bring weariness to the speaker. We can hear a similar sense of such inevitability in Nathaniel Mackey's take on Jean Toomer's *Cane*. *Cane*, Mackey argues, "portrays its own predicament," and thus "shows that music or poetry, if not exactly a loser's art, is fed by an intimacy with loss and may in fact feed it."[11] In his assessment Mackey captures something important about representation more generally, for what he reads in Toomer's struggle to make art out of loss is not unlike the struggle foaming just beneath the surface of Kaufman's poem. If we imagine each of these artists, Proust, Toomer, Kaufman, and many of the authors who have appeared in this book, if we imagine these artists as in some way using writing to expiate their blues, to illuminate and perhaps bring closure to their still-vibrating, unfinished encounters, then we must also imagine that in the process of revisitation such artists must also face the fact that their art might bring that loss into a more full ownership, closer.

When Proust's narrator is left to deal with the reverberation of his first re-encounter with the madeleine, its shivery effect, he also soon realizes that locating the origin of that sensation means making himself again vulnerable to the circumstances crystallized in that effect. His remembering, played out simultaneously as a journey to and also as an inhabitation of the world of his past, is in the writing process drawn from inside himself, filling the room, making the novel. In this case, the intimacy with loss inherent in the very process of remembering the past is indeed desirable, for what might have happened to Proust's narrator if he had not so carefully meditated upon the origin of that singular sensation, the vague shimmer of remembrance that comes to him in the tea-touched madeleine's taste? If he had been unable to ground it, unable to substantiate and therefore reclaim the meaning of the sensation, he would had been made prisoner to it, doomed to a melancholic reiteration without remembrance. And *Swann's Way*? A ghost story rather than a memory story. But what are the terms of engagement in cases where such inhabitation, even in the interest of expiation, might indeed come at too high a cost? There is more than a little bit of this in Kaufman's poem, displayed as a murmuring ambivalence on the cost of battle, despite such battles having been revealed as only about himself, foundational *to* himself. This must be why, as the poem expresses in its closing couplet, "The tragedies are sung nightly at the funerals of the poet; / The revisited soul is wrapped in the aura of familiarity."

CAROLING, SOFTLY

"Caroling softly," Jean Toomer's "Song of the Son" communicates a deep ambivalence, mainly through its evocation of Southern blacks as a beautiful and terrible people living in an equally beautiful and terrible natural world, each reflecting upon the other with a destructive and redolent symmetry. Indeed, throughout Toomer's *Cane* readers are often set in the midst of such mutually sustaining encroachments. Appearing in *Cane*'s first section, "Song of the Son" speaks to Toomer's desire to preserve the beauty of a time and place in its fade, to create what historian Pierre Nora refers to as *le milieu*—"a real environment of memory."[12] Its theorization of its own memorializing impulse puts the poem in a particularly revealing relationship to *Cane* more generally. At first glance, the poem shares much with *Cane*'s aesthetically imbricated, yet emotionally detached narration. Closer analysis, however, shows how this detachment might in fact mask quite the opposite, reveals it as an aesthetic response to an affective terror, itself coming out of an uncomfortable identification with a previously sought-after object. Even as the poem's structure mimics a kind of spectatorship common to the prose pieces that make up the book's first section, "Song of the Son" watches itself watching, and thus also accounts for what might be at stake in such watching and seeking. In "Song of the Son" insight comes at a terrible cost to the artist as his attempt to draw closer to the past instead reveals the encroachment of that past on his future.

The poem's five stanzas tell the story of an artist turning to the South as a repository of his cultural past. Moving in three consecutive parts, it systematically shifts across voices and temporalities: an atemporal and omniscient opening invocation, an interrupted ode that responds to the invocation from a heroic perspective, and then a sudden break, out of which the hero emerges humble and grounded. It begins:

> POUR O pour that parting soul in song,
> O pour it in the sawdust glow of night,
> Into the velvet pine-smoke air to-night,
> And let the valley carry it along.
> And let the valley carry it along.
>
> (1–5)[13]

With its address to no one and its situation in a virtual present, the poem's opening lines stage the poem's narrative in an epic or mythic space. This sense of the mythic or epic is strengthened by the clarity of the command, "Pour O pour," coupled with the absence of an object of address. Here, the object of address can only come into being through the command, in response to the call: who would step up to answer this call? Who might make this song? Further, the poem's replication of imagery from other texts in *Cane*—sawdust glow and pine-smoke air—contributes to a sense that the poem's lines come from anywhere and nowhere, bringing meaning to this poem through its representation of other times and spaces in *Cane*. Full, this voice carries a special authority, the kind of authority given to common knowledge, to folklore, to God. Closest to such godliness, the final two lines of the stanza, clean and clear, generate a lyrical, soft, and comforting identity: "And let the valley carry it along./ And let the valley carry it along."

With its next two stanzas, Toomer's poem begins again, this time from the perspective of a speaking "I," a new speaker whose arrival is inevitably situated in response to the challenge put forth in the invocation. His language is big, trying to meet the invocation in its own terms, on its register:

> O land and soil, red soil and sweet-gum tree,
> So scant of grass, so profligate of pines,
> Now just before an epoch's sun declines
> Thy son, in time, I have returned to thee,
> Thy son, I have in time returned to thee.
>
> (6–10)

Not a redundancy, this speaker's apostrophe to "land and soil" highlights the spatial dimension in Toomer's ode, not only drawing attention to the landscape itself but also to a larger sense of place attached to land, to notions of homeland and nation here etched by the affection one hears in the materiality of the speaker's address. This sense of place is also strengthened in the stanza's final lines, in which the speaker announces his own return. He is *the* son, a savior returning at twilight in order to memorialize this place in its fade and dissolve.

In both stanzas, Toomer foregrounds time, urgency, as the poem's narrator insists in his address that his late arrival will not prevent him from fulfilling his task, which is to meet the demand set forth in the poem's opening invocation:

> In time, for though the sun is setting on
> A song-lit race of slaves, it has not set;
> Though late, O soil, it is not too late yet
> To catch thy plaintive soul, leaving, soon gone,
> Leaving, to catch thy plaintive soul soon gone.
>
> (11–15)

Here, the poem's temporality is staged in relation to the group whom we must assume the poem is interested in, the "song-lit race of slaves" whose spirit must be caught before "an epoch's sun declines." This claim is straightforward, framed by a familiar discourse of historical change and articulated in a well-known language concerned with the passing of generations and the preservation of the past for the future. In many ways, the speaker's language in the second and third stanzas is not unlike that of the invocation, visually and sonically reminded to us in the "O" of his own address.

Yet despite this resonance with the mythical, neither stanzas' final lines can quite achieve the sweet repetition available to whomever or whatever has chanted the poem's opening invocation. There is something missing, as Toomer's use of chiasmus in the final lines of each of these two stanzas casts suspicion on the authority of the speaker's address. Chiastic structures create a kind of mirroring in texts, reversing one set of terms or concepts in relation to another and thus generating fresh meaning through the play on sameness and difference. In the first instance the mirror's placement—the site or center of the reflection, the center of the crossmark—is made heavy by the repetition of terms or concepts. A straight take on Toomer's syntactical use of chiasmus in the second stanza would thus look like this:

> Thy son, | in time, I have | returned to thee,
> ×
> Thy son, | I have in time | returned to thee.
>
> (9–10)

Toomer's use of chiasmus deepens the resonance of what might otherwise be experienced by the reader as a sheer repetition, might otherwise cruise by as an identity structure not unlike the lyrically soothing closing couplet of the poem's opening invocation, "And let the valley carry it along,/ And let the valley carry it along." Here, the chiastic structure of the lines builds an emotional momentum around the urgency of this arrival. The return? It is a given, stable and redundant in its facticity. But who might *actually* take the place of the son, and *would* he arrive in time. Such questions offer a potential for crisis in the poem. In the first line, the timeliness of his arrival is subordinated to the fact of return; however the second line brings a new assertion to the first, foregrounding both the son's timeliness and the fact of himself, his "I."

I AND THOU AT THE CROSSROADS

It is strange, however, that despite the strength of this I, there is no direct communication between the son and his forbearers. Much as the stanza's final lines cannot quite achieve the sweet repetition that consolidates the invocation, there is also something suspicious in the speaker's deferral of the I. Referring to himself as "Thy son" places the personal at a distance from the event of return and splits the subject into two—the son and he who returns the son. Further, the origin of this material that the returned son has taken responsibility for making into art has also been split. Despite the familiarity one might assume from his asserted relation, "Thy son," *your son*, the poem is in fact addressed to the land and not to its people. On the one hand there is nothing unusual in this, particularly as the grandiloquence of the son's address is well suited to such an abstraction; again, the *thys* and *thees*, the son and his homeland. But, at the same time, choosing such an address complicates the otherwise heavily avowed relation. For even as the speaker's apostrophe forefronts the fact of return to his homeland, the constitution of that land as an object of address edges its own kind of violence, as it not only removes Southern blacks from a certain kind of subject position, as mothers and fathers to the son, but also substitutes an otherwise inanimate object into that position. Despite the *thy* and *thee* cant of Toomer's poem, there is no proper "thou" in the speaker's address.

As Barbara Johnson points out, such shifting is endemic to apostrophe in general, and in its value is attached to a certain kind of power relationship:

> Apostrophe is thus both direct and indirect: based etymologically on the notion of turning aside, of digressing from straight speech, it manipulates the I/Thou structure of direct address in an indirect, fictionalized way. The absent, dead, or inanimate entity addressed is thereby made present, animate, and anthropomorphic. Apostrophe is a form of

> ventriloquism through which the speaker throws voice, life, and human form into the addressee, turning its silence into mute responsiveness.[14]

The son's address, which brings life to the soil, consolidates some of the meaning inherent in the poem's fertile and nature-bound imagery by setting the stage for the narrator's return as an opportunity for rebirth, for the "one seed" that will become "an everlasting song, a singing tree," as prophesied in the poem's closing. One must, however, wonder at what cost comes this opportunity for renewal, especially as the poem repeatedly shadows the speaker's optimism in his project, thus suggesting that the terms of his return might be different from what he has imagined.

If we return to the beginning of the son's address, for instance, the speaker's transfer of address to the soil technically makes his return as much to the soil and trees as it is to the place, a return to the land *per se*. If that is the case, then this journey is not necessarily a return to the soil as home, a fertile or recuperative narrative; this is a return to the dust, a death narrative. We thus find at the heart of "Song of the Son" a profound problematic: the death at hand on the poem's surface may be that of the Southern black folk, but at stake in the son's memorialization of their passing is the realization of the possibility of his own death. In this reading, the timeliness that emerges at the center of that chiastic first statement would thus mark the site of his burial, an intimation of the narrator's death that becomes more apparent at the end of the second half of the speaker's address:

> To catch thy plaintive soul, leaving, I soon gone,
>
> ✕
>
> Leaving, to catch thy plaintive soul I soon gone.
>
> (15–16)

This time, Toomer's use of chiasmus transposes the speaker with the plaintive souls, in the second sentence describing the speaker as leaving despite having already attached that leaving to the plaintive soul. The meaning of this transposition is ultimately consolidated by the couplet's now haunting boundary—be it the son or the soul, it is soon gone.

The poem has shifted, and what at first seemed only a variation in address is thus revealed as something more pervasive. It is as if the narrator cannot recover from this new knowledge, and, similarly, the poem itself can no longer hold its form, as its heroic stance is temporally destabilized, interrupted by this new address. Such destabilization had in fact been present all along: if we assume that "Song of the Son" reflects the historical moment of *Cane*'s writing, which is simply to say that the poem is posited in Toomer's own writerly present, then the speaker's address to the Negro slaves is fundamentally anachronistic. Slavery has ended; they are not in the present of the narrative, even as this stanza is so cast. His land is a place of death.

This is further and again confirmed in the middle of the next stanza, in another and equally radical temporal shift: between the second and third lines the narration changes, stuttering the tempo and removing vigor from the speaker's narration. One moment the speaker is at arm's distance, addressing the Negro slaves "squeezed" and "bursting," up in "the pine-wood air,"—subject and object, I and thou. Then a sudden shift into the personal and present: "Passing, before they stripped the old tree bare/ One plum was saved for me"—subject becomes object, the bearer of a received meaning comes into being through that which has been given to him, that which has been passed on to him. This sudden recognition of goneness is also signified on the surface of the text as a break in form, as in its content the poem's next stanza transfers the object of address from soil to Negro and in its form diverges from the ABBCC rhyme scheme of the previous stanzas, losing a line in the process:

> O Negro slaves, dark purple ripened plums,
> Squeezed, and bursting in the pine-wood air,
> Passing, before they stripped the old tree bare
> One plum was saved for me, one seed becomes
> An everlasting song, a singing tree,
> Caroling softly souls of slavery,
> What they were, and what they are to me,
> Caroling softly souls of slavery.
>
> (16–24)

As Charles Scruggs points out, even as the poem moves to resolution, to a fulfillment of the invocation's mission, its meaning is also irrevocability tainted by Southern violence: "Thus art is to redeem history, but the metaphor of purple plums on a tree, 'bursting in the pine-wood air,' hints of something more sinister than redemption."[15] Arriving at a crossroads, not of decision but of realization, the speaker in his reception of the seed crosses a series of boundaries, the temporal boundaries already named as well as his crossing over from subject to object, a move foreshadowed in the insight into his own mortality. Cross-referenced, cross-addressed, cross-purposed: although never explicitly named in "Song of the Son," crosses abound in Toomer's poem. Each enables the next: the crossing of the spatial with the temporal; the crossroads of consciousness to which the speaker is brought in the course of the poem and that is itself revealed as a crossroad between the living and the dead; the chiastic structure of that revelation. Further, the cross appears in the Christian imagery attached to the speaker's struggle, to his return as a prodigal son and also in his bearing of this cross, of this sacrificial legacy. Indeed, the very thematic of the poem, which is fundamentally based in the passing of the black folk, could also be said to rewrite the fifth station of the cross, in its depiction of that people's final hours, in its scene of death and suffering.[16]

The poem's last line, rocking, gently mocking—sardonic—echoes its opening. The son has found what he is looking for. *Pungent and composite, the Dixie Pike has grown from goat path in Africa.*[17] But what does it mean to return to this place, to this land, to this Southern place of great beauty but also of pain and terror? A place of bodies dark and ripe, but also squeezed and bursting, murdered. When the lynching narrative emerges in "Song of the Son," the speaker suddenly realizes that it had in fact been there all along, waiting for him: faithful, unflinching, and holding in "the tiny and almost impalpable drop of its essence, the vast structure of recollection." Ironically fortunate, he will limp away with a phantom pain, humbled and readied, bearing the cross.[18]

5 Saying "Yes" in *Kindred*

> Like other kinds of pain, phantom pain is a phenomenon known but not understood by medical professionals. Unlike other types of pain, no body part need be present for it to occur. Felt by amputees, it is an apparition, a ghost thought to exist only in the mind, as a memory unforgotten. But then, the problem with pain altogether is its invisibility. Maybe most pain is phantom pain. . . . Subjective and suffered in a world and time of objective medicine, its existence does not always rely on a light spot, a shadow on an X-ray, or the frank evidence of blood. It belongs to the world hidden inside a boot, to secret histories of inner worlds, to beds where the sick are unseen, beds where human mystery, wounding, and love occur.[1]
>
> —Linda Hogan

I remember the first time I taught Joy Kogawa's *Obasan*. It was an introductory literature course, one of those survey classes many college students take. It was our first day back after Spring Break, and in a class of nearly forty students, maybe ten had read the book. Determined to have a productive class, I put them into groups, where they had to come up with one example of an aspect of American history that had been excluded from the national narratives they had learned in high school. It was an incredibly diverse class, and I figured that each group would find it a challenge to agree on which story "deserved" to be told. The idea was that 1) it was a backdoor way to get them thinking about history, memory, and counter-memory, and 2) the diverse investments of each group member would make it difficult for the groups to themselves agree on a single example, thus illustrating some of the political relations between community memory, national history, and individual identity.

The groups were chugging along, and what I must admit began as a somewhat punitive exercise had become quite exciting and productive—though one of the groups was having more fun than group-work should ever produce. Two of the group's members were in the midst of one of their elaborate comedy routines, this time reproducing their own version of the then oft-run television commercials for Colonial Williamsburg. Every commercial follows the same format: some child from the present meets some child from Colonial Williamsburg, who is always playing with some sort of eighteenth-century hoop and stick-type toy. Colonial girl says, in her vaguely accented English from the past, "Would you like to play with my hoop?" The two children are matched in age, gender, race, and appearance, the only difference being their styles of dress, and of course, the lame toy. Suddenly, twentieth-century child, ready to conquer the alien object, takes the hoop, and (gasp) hula-hoops! The Williamsburg child is shocked and amazed, for of course we are supposed to believe that she is not a fictional character, and that Colonial Williamsburg is not merely a museum, but really a journey back through time. My local comedians had latched onto this last point and, departing from the notion that this could really be an encounter between children from different centuries, explored a simple proposition: what if the children were black? "Hello. Would you like to go pick some cotton with me?"; "Hey! You dere wanna play wit my shackles?"—and so on the shtick went. I am sure you can imagine. But with that simple joke, they had exposed the myth of Colonial Williamsburg, or perhaps more specifically, had reminded their classmates of the whitewashing necessary to making history commercially viable, commodifiable, in the present.

We laughed long and hard that day, indulging fully in the wry, almost tearful laughter that only a contest between insight and bitterness can bring. At the end of the day laughter usually chases such bitterness away, but I cannot help but wonder if any of us could have really identified the bitter root, despite the efficacy of our ritual expiation. Did it come from the fact that something akin to my students' version of history would never be included in a national narrative? Or from the fact that the absence of such stories do not make them any less real in their meaning to the present? Sardonic, ironic, we were jammed in the space between our indignation at being absented and the pain that sometimes comes with bringing the self back into recognition. Days later, as we finished *Obasan*, we talked about how neglected histories may sometimes go untold not only because "history is for the winners," or because history operates in the service of a national political majority, but also because, sometimes, people cannot bear to tell such stories or to re-live such lives. The question, "Would you like to pick some cotton?" takes away historical wonder, takes away the possibility of play and enchantment with the past—for who could ever say "yes"?

The problem of the "yes," of affirming an historical identity that is potentially harmful to oneself, troubles some of the imaginative leaps necessary to students' processes of identification when reading, for if the most common rationale for representing violent and troubling histories is so that "we may learn from the past," how do we account for students' refusals to see themselves in such pasts? On some level I take issue with the notion that a reader is supposed to identify with a text in order to "enjoy" it, but when students, who very often begin their reading from the point of identification, avoid it, I cannot help but be intrigued. When teaching slave narratives, for instance, I am always struck by how students generally protect themselves from the texts, usually either by claiming deep admiration for the slave-protagonist, "She is *so* amazing. I *never* would have survived slavery," or by asserting their own necessarily acontextualized resistance: "That never would have been me. I would've killed somebody." As Lisa Long notes:

> as student responses to these novels indicate, contemporary Americans—both white and African American . . . all want to imagine that we would be the defiant and brave African American slave or white Underground Railroad worker. We would not be the ones maimed or killed—surely not the ones doing the maiming and killing.[2]

In my own experiences of teaching slave narratives, I have often come up against the resistance that Long describes, though I must admit that I cannot recall a single instance when a student has willingly engaged with even the "good" white characters, much less engaged in an extended recognition of an aggressor or oppressor who could not in some way claim a victim status. It is typical for students to avoid identifications with slaves, but absolutely taboo for them to think too deeply about the slaveholders. If I am not careful, white people, except as a sort of shadowy, menacing force, are actively disappeared from class discussions. They are simply too difficult to deal with outside of their caricatures. Some of this, I think, has to do with classroom dynamics, with students' fears of slipping down the slopes of racial discourse: explanation, insofar as it tends towards understanding, puts one at risk of outing oneself as a sympathizer with an oppressor—an outcome made even more risky in racially diverse or predominately white classrooms. This hesitation is on a certain level sensible; scholars as well often rear up before the possibility of a dangerous identification. Even if the students do not know why, they know that slavery and its proponents must be condemned, which is of course a reasonable and even "right" response. But, at the same time, not confronting oppressors, or even more specifically, not allowing oneself even for a moment to identify with an oppressor, potentially keeps one cloaked from one's own horrible potentiality.

This helps us get at something about the scope of Sethe's crime in *Beloved*: when she kills her child, she acts as an absolute authority, carrying out a mandate she imagines as validated by history, as if she could be absolved prior to her act. But at the moment of her murdering, Sethe's dominion over her children's lives is not unlike that of a slaveholder, for it is specifically an enactment of dominion over their flesh. A mother might recite to her child: "I brought you into this world, and I can take you out of it," but the sentiment, allegorical, is quite the opposite of what it says—it is a gesture of protection. Sethe's act is complete in its signification, for it actualizes that which should only be spoken. The shocking absolutism of the event traumatizes Baby Suggs, undoing all she had tried to recuperate vis-à-vis her ministry of love for the flesh, which is synonymous with its reclamation from dominion. When Stamp Paid, later, tries to coax a conversation about the event out of Baby Suggs, all she can reply is that

"They came into my yard," a statement that refers to more than the literal arrival of Schoolteacher and his men, just as "yard" means more than dirt and grass. For Baby Suggs, the literalness of Sethe's act collapses the gap between sign and signifier. Color can only name color: "there ain't no bad luck in this world but whitefolks."[3]

Indeed, Long's last point, that "we" would "surely" never be the "ones doing the maiming and killing," is critical, for even as any act of speaking for a victim—of putting oneself in the place of the victim—is fraught with the dangers of appropriative empathy or of painful haunting, speaking for an aggressor can be far more dangerous, as perhaps there is nothing more troubling than an even transitory identification with someone whom you would like to claim your soul speaks against. To do so is transgressive. But, at the same time, allowing ourselves to always identify only with victims not only undermines the very idea that troubling histories must live on for their learning, it also makes the doers of violence shadowy and elusive aberrations, spared the repudiation that comes with an actively rejected identification, having instead been absented from the very discourse their actions have engendered.[4] This absenting of the perpetrator can also lead to a fundamental misconception, to a sense that the perpetrators of the world's great crimes somehow came unto their victims from elsewhere, that every instance of violence of whites against blacks during slavery, for instance, somehow reenacted the landing of Europeans on the African coast. The truth of American slavery, of course, is quite the opposite, as victims and perpetrators are seldom, if ever, alien to each other.

ALIEN ENCOUNTERS

What genre, then, is more suited to exploding the myth of alien encounter than science fiction? Science fiction, so often misunderstood as the province of white men and their green aliens, offers a freedom of exploration useful to the task of thematizing some of the more haunting aspects of black experience in the Americas. Not only is the genre appropriate to the task of articulating slips and slides in spatial and temporal existence, but it also makes possible new kinds of first person narratives, as the genre's oldest device, time travel, allows protagonists to experience historical moments as present phenomena, to incarnate history by literally inhabiting the space of the past. Such is the case with Octavia Butler's *Kindred*, a novel that uses time travel to map the often uncanny interlocutions of race, gender, and history.

Kindred is mostly Dana's story. Dana, a newly married black woman in 1970s Los Angeles, works as a temp, awaiting her big break as a writer. She is our protagonist *cum* tour guide, our girl with the hoop. The day Dana and her husband Kevin, white and also a writer, move into their new house, she falls to the floor, dizzy. When she awakens, she finds herself in antebellum Maryland. The first thing she sees is a drowning child, and, instinctively, she saves his life. When the boy's father arrives, he threatens her with a shotgun and, suddenly, she is transported, wet and muddy, back to her present.[5] This scene at the river is the first of many times Dana will be called to save Rufus Weylin's life, and the only way she can return to her present is to believe she is dying; though, inevitably, she will always be returned to the past, each time to save Rufus' life—which she must do. For even though Rufus is the white child of a plantation owner, and when in the past Dana occupies the position of his slave, he is also her ancestor, a distant grandfather, and it is such that Dana's obligation to Rufus' life, which is also an obligation to her own, structures the interplay of history and morality that motivates Butler's plot. If Rufus dies, Dana will never be born. Or rather, she cannot afford to find out what would happen to her if she were not to save him. By putting Dana in this dilemma, Butler is able to illustrate the deep and thorny entanglement at the heart of Southern plantation slavery, thus undoing any cultural myth of alien encounter. Further, by structuring the text around Dana's various obligations to life (her own, Rufus', other slaves'), Butler not only complicates the range of Dana's responses in any situation, but she also forces the reader to abide by the same rules.

The idea that different worlds abide by different rules is fundamental to science fiction, as it assures the comprehensibility of alien times and spaces, thus convincing the reader that what transpires in the text is possible by allowing him or her to understand the very specific contours of that place and time, no matter how experientially distant that place would otherwise seem to the reader. In *Kindred,* Butler uses science fiction's often hyperbolic stance—the genre's de facto commitment to writing from the limit of more regularly perceived experiences—to illuminate how people could have survived in a world dedicated to what Keith Gilyard has referred to as "the devoicing and identity-eradicating imperatives of masters and overseers."[6] In an interview with Charles Rowell, Butler recalls:

> I was occasionally taken to work with my mother and made to sit in the car all day, because I wasn't really welcome inside, of course. Sometimes, I was able to go inside and hear people talk about or to my mother in ways that were obviously disrespectful. As a child I did not blame them for their disgusting behavior, but I blamed my mother for taking it. I didn't really understand. This is something I carried with me for quite a while, as she entered back doors, and as she went deaf at appropriate times. If she had heard more, she would have had to react to it, you know. The usual.[7]

When we say that we carry something with us, we often mean that we have brought into ourselves a burden someone else has given, a shaming. I imagine this thing that Butler carried with her "for quite a while" as a potent admixture of shame and anger, and as indicative of a generational gap widened by ideological transformations surfaced in the wake of the Civil Rights and Black Power movements. Every slight her mother seemingly ignores or, even worse, doesn't seem to mind, recapitulates Butler's anger. More than one black child has experienced this with parents or grandparents, this seeming deference to whiteness that is painful to watch and is in its tenor unfamiliar to his or her own experience of race. Butler, however, did have an explanation for her mother's behavior: "If she had heard more, she would have had to react to it, you know. The usual." Here Butler's recollection hints at her understandably overdetermined assessment of her mother's situation, for it is clear that she had not come to it by observing her mother solely in terms of her real predicament, in terms of her mother's relation to their survival: "I wasn't really welcome inside, of course"; "you know"; "the usual": *as seen on TV*, as written in books. *You know*, the cultural memory; *you know, of course, the usual* way these things go.

But then, Butler adds,

> . . . as I got older I realized that this is what kept me fed, and this is what kept a roof over my head. This is when I started to pay attention to what my mother and even more my grandmother and my poor great-grandmother, who died as a very young woman giving birth to my grandmother, what they all went through.

Butler's matured relationship to the realities of survival moves her from condemnation to sympathy: "what they all went through"; "my poor great-grandmother." And, by attending to those who have attended to the necessities of her own life, Butler comes to understand the specificity of their experiences of the world, their rules of survival. Even as she cannot know exactly what they went through, she *can* comprehend that they went as best as they knew how. This knowledge, despite its limits, lessens shame's burden and enables the transfer of her own anger to its proper object, to the "disgusting behavior" of the white employers.

Improving the lens through which her audience considers the past is an important part of Butler's project, as she attempts to make her readers, perhaps even black readers specifically, understand that in the same situation, they may not have done any differently than their ancestors. With this in mind, *Kindred* was first conceived as a pedagogical project:

> When I got into college, Pasadena City College, the black nationalist movement, the Black Power Movement, was really underway with the young people, and I heard some remarks from a young man who was the same age I was but who had apparently never made the connection with what his parents did to keep him alive. He was still blaming them for their humility and their acceptance of disgusting behavior on the part of employers and other people. He said, "I'd like to kill all these

> old people who have been holding us back for so long. But I can't because I'd have to start with my own parents." When he said *us* he meant black people, and when he said *old people* he meant older black people. That was actually the germ of the idea for *Kindred* (1979). I've carried that comment with me for thirty years. He felt so strongly ashamed of what the older generation had to do, without really putting it into the context of being necessary for not only their lives but his as well.

The problems and sorrows of living in the world grate against the monumentalizing tendencies of progressive revolutionary thought, particularly as popular revolutions are often at some level revolts against an historical shame, against a haunting that can only be expiated in death. But because Butler has come into a different and new understanding of her generation's relation to its ancestors, she is in fact shamed by her peer's shame, which had been expressed in this instance as a destructive, killing rage. Shame always hearkens towards death, as the shamed believes that only death can erase the mark; *I was so ashamed, I wanted to die right on the spot*: "I'd like to kill all these old black people who have been holding us back for so long." Nevertheless, to kill one's ancestors is to kill oneself, and it is this dilemma, made extravagantly literal, that *Kindred* tackles. With *Kindred*, Butler works towards a strategy for passing on painful histories, as enacting the possibilities of world-making in literature is no small feat for texts that need their readers to engage the life-experiences of people who have suffered as many never will, particularly when that suffering implicates people with whom readers can identify—their own ancestors laid bare as *people*, as the subjects and objects of history. Dana's haunting experience of the past as the present is an experience of pain, horror, and disillusionment, coming at a nearly unsustainable cost. It is in this way that texts like *Kindred*, and neo-slave narratives more generally, attempt to move specific histories away from the silent and shameful not by representing history—that would be the work of historical fiction—but rather by bringing the historical past into the present tense, thus conjuring history's actualities—flesh, survival, and the things people do in the interest of the future. Such texts make readerly identification possible by making manageable the shame of one's encounter with the past. By creating a space where one can say yes, such encounters teach us how many have made the transition from victim to survivor.[8]

SCREENED HISTORY

In *Kindred*, there is a sense that Butler has come to this knowledge through her own reading, for her reading seems very much on the surface of the text. As Robert Crossley has pointed out, the specters of the more heavily circulated slave narratives, like those of Frederick Douglass and Harriet

Jacobs, bob and weave from beginning to end of Butler's own narrative.[9] Of course the idea that an author has culled the raw materials of her own fiction-making from other literary sources is hardly new or interesting, but something about Butler's writing suggests that her production of *Kindred* perhaps worked as its own kind of salve, that the book was written to negotiate her own experiences of reading and consequently being haunted by slave narratives. That what began as a pedagogical project has for its author become a therapeutic one.

Butler makes sure that we understand that reading and writing hold a central place in *Kindred*. Dana's first travel to Maryland, for instance, occurs when she, frustrated that she is stuck with housework while her husband Kevin gets to write, is unpacking their books into their new house.[10] There is something important in this moment as Dana, her hands on her books and her emotions revolving around her indignation, is momentarily suspended between her familiar, chosen life as a writer and her unfamiliar and unchosen role as a domestic. Butler immediately concretizes the uncanny sensation, as she makes the briefly unfamiliar domestic present double as the site of an unfamiliar domestic past, a slippery traversion made possible by the convergence of race, gender, and history—a convergence which, once revealed, resituates Dana's home as a place of danger and vulnerability: "I feel like it could happen again," she confesses, "—like it could happen anytime. I don't feel secure here."[11] As Crossley notes:

> Shuttling between the two white men in her life, she is aware not only of the blood link between herself and Rufus but of the double link of gender and race that unites Rufus and Kevin. The convergence of these two white men in Dana's life not only dramatizes the ease with which even a 'progressive' white man falls into the cultural pattern of dominance, but suggests as well an uncanny synonymy of the words 'husband' and 'master.'[12]

In the past, Rufus enlists Dana as his amanuensis, which is painful both because it denudes Dana's passion for writing and also because it reminds her of Kevin's previous attempts to get her to do the same in their present.[13] Though they are both writers by trade, Kevin is the primary breadwinner, having recently had more luck publishing than Dana. Later in the novel, when Rufus asks Dana to take care of some of his work, it would almost be humorous, if the circumstances were not so dire, the implications so horrifying. Her experience of involuntary service catapults Dana into a past that is unfamiliar and also hers. As its haunting of her present emerges more fully into consciousness, her present is transformed into that past. Rather than leaving it in the past, she returns to it time and time again.

It is important that such return in not limited to Dana, for Butler makes it clear that this transportation is available to anyone with the right kind of access to the right kind of text. After Dana returns from the past the second time, she and Kevin begin collecting and devouring every book they can acquire about slavery, delving in with a passion that would seem obsessive if it were not for the special circumstances of Dana's time travel. They are determined that if she must go, then at least she could be as educated as possible about the time space to which she travels. When her transportations first began, Dana was more familiar with the literature and history of slavery than Kevin. But when faced with Dana's travel, Kevin works hard to learn more about the specificities of her predicament, an effort Butler validates—for lack of a better term—with a trip to the past with Dana. It is important, however, that Kevin can only time-travel if he is touching Dana, thus suggesting that *she* is in fact the text that matters. One night, Rufus tells her about a moment when he briefly saw her in *her* present, "I saw you inside a room. I could see part of the room, and there were books all around."[14] By literally making Dana's body a text, that which holds the narrative, Butler suggests one can only travel to a past about which one has a prior memory-sense, through which one is already haunted.

It is around notions of reading, writing, and education that we thus find *Kindred*'s central paradox. In her novel Butler creates for us a world in which the comprehension of history is only possible in bodily, actualized experience—even as the conditions for such experiences are consolidated in her characters' acts of reading, through reading books that can never themselves approximate the lived experiences on which they are based. In *Kindred*, this paradox is played out as a radical temporal disjuncture between the two timespaces. When Dana and Kevin are together in either timespace, they experience time in the same way. But when only one is in 1815, for instance, the one left behind in 1976 experiences the other's absence as roughly equivalent to the amount of time it would have taken for him or her to read about what transpired in the other's life in the past, thus illustrating within *Kindred* the difference between the time of living and the time of reading. What to Dana feels like two hours in 1815 feels like just minutes to Kevin, feels just as long as it would take to read this page.

Through her constant reiteration of this temporal disjuncture, Butler insists that there is no possibility for an experience of the past outside of first-person experience, for even time, relative to the individual, refuses synchronicity in spite of any notion of a reader coming to knowledge through story. The author can never herself touch the life of her protagonist, and like her own reader she is thus inadequate to the task of writing. If one were to believe *Kindred*'s theorization of its own terms, Butler would in fact be nothing more than an amanuensis to the past, merely transcribing the past as it transpires. And indeed, such privileging of daily, bodily, lived experience is central to the African-American expressive tradition: *Shit is real. The real deal. That's keeping it real.* Nevertheless, this idea that one must physically experience history in order to have any knowledge of it puts at risk the very idea of reading and writing about the past. Even Dana herself, recently returned from Maryland, realizes that "As real as the whole episode was, as real as I know it was, it's beginning to recede from me somehow. It's becoming like something I saw on television or read about—like something I got second hand."[15]

Despite the ways Butler foregrounds reading, it is important to note that when Dana arrives in the past, she soon learns that her own education, including her book learning, her reading, and the movies she has seen, are inadequate to the task of actually living in an unfamiliar time and space: "I had seen people beaten on television and in the movies. I had seen the too-red blood substitute streaked across their backs and heard their well-rehearsed screams. But I hadn't lain nearby and smelled their sweat or heard them pleading and praying, shamed before their friends and themselves."[16] Despite the voraciousness of her reading, Dana finds herself profoundly unfamiliar with the everyday things that go unglossed, including the extraordinary event of escape, one of the most notably undocumented aspects of slave life. After she is captured in her attempted escape, she admits "I knew about towns and rivers miles away—and it hadn't done me a damned bit of good! What had Weylin said? That educated didn't mean smart. He had a point. Nothing in my education or knowledge of the future had helped me escape." Immediately, however, history comes to recoup at least a little bit of Dana's loss: "Yet in a few years an illiterate runaway named Harriet Tubman would make nineteen trips into this country and lead three hundred fugitives to freedom."[17] Dana, severely beaten and failed in her escape attempt, turns to the past's future, her other history, for comfort. In terms of flow, this moment is one of *Kindred*'s choppiest, if not actually insensible, moments. Neither narratively nor emotionally does the statement fit the text's momentum, but it is nonetheless an absolutely fascinating moment because it marks Butler's attempt to recuperate personal loss via historical citation. On the level of the text, this replacement feels like an intrusion, the place where, if Dana were on a therapist's couch, one would find an obdurate screen memory, a psychic panacea that attempts to move the reader away from the truth of the protagonist's reality. In this way, *Kindred* is situated between reading's virtual satisfactions and the limits of such satisfaction. Through her experience, Dana comes into memory while we, mere readers, are left only with history, really finding ourselves in the text only through our sympathy with Dana's dissatisfaction with her own book learning.

WRITTEN IN THE BODY

What does it mean to say that an author cannot touch the life of her protagonist, even as the protagonist of course has nothing that could properly be referred as a life outside of the author? And what does this mean for a text like *Kindred*, which one may understand as a text written in its author's attempt to come to terms with her own relationship to a painful past? To get at this, it may help to turn for a moment to *Kindred*'s central rule—Dana's obligation to life, which dictates that she can only return to her proper contemporary life when she believes she is dying. This mandate forms the second half of the ricochet motion that shuttles her between the two timespaces, the first half of course being the fact of Rufus' endangerment, which calls her to him whenever he believes that he is dying. In this way, her transportation is thus mechanized by either character's encounter with an absolute limit. Dana's experience of being transported between two distinct times and places by the fear of her own death resonates with therapist and anthropologist Roberta Culbertson's description of the spatial and temporal splitting experienced by people in instances of repeated and violent violation, experiences that are often later described by her patients as remembered experiences of faraway places inaccessible to anyone except them. In such places, tormentors are actually monsters and bedrooms might become dungeons, for instance, for through wounding the body is projected into a different time and space, a time and space away from other people and daily life. As Culbertson wants us to understand, these places are not metaphorical, for they have been literally experienced. They are places with their own experiential rules and boundaries, not beholden to conventional distinctions between the real and the fake, the material and the hallucinatory. "No experience is more one's own that harm to one's own skin," Culbertson tells us, "but none is more locked within that skin, . . . *Trapped there, the violation seems to continue in a reverberating present that belies the supposed linearity of time and the possibility of endings*."[18] In such a circumstance, telling becomes less a problem of language and more a problem of time and space, a problem of the listener's inability to comprehend the contours of a distant place to which no one but the speaker will ever travel.

In Culbertson's analysis, this distance is measured on a scale of inaccessibility, by the relative possibility of an experience's emergence from a deep interiority and thus the possibility of its meaning in a shared world. Indeed, much as it is important not to mistake a survivor's language as metaphorical, because metaphor presumes distance between sign and signified, it is problematic to conceptualize this as a matter of distance because in the cases Culbertson works with all distances have collapsed, the signified *is* the sign, and the collapse of this distance changes the meaning of difference in the world:

> . . . the memory of trauma, or the knowledge of things past, is not merely of a wild and skewed time inaccessible except on its own terms, either in 'flashbacks' or 'neuroses' or in the form of the numb survivor self, but also the memory of other levels of reality, sensed not even by the five senses, *but by the body itself, or by the spiritual mind, the interior of the body*. This sort of memory is without language, perhaps without image. When such gross tools as language are brought to bear

> on the experience, the result appears to be metaphor, but it is not. As Terrence Des Pres says, in circumstances of extremity, 'symbols tend to actualize.'[19]

Despite the resonance Culbertson's assessment carries with Proust, here putting knowledge in the place of remembrance, it is important that here even sensation does not offer passage from memory to consciousness, which thus makes it possible for the body to haunt what is generally regarded as the self. Simultaneous with this haunting also comes an intimation of the extent to which the traumatic can never come to function as an historical, for there is no possibility for dissemination.

What we should take from this, however, is not quite about the impossibility of understanding the traumatic; rather what comes of this is something important about the temporality of knowledge more generally. As Henri Bergson notes:

> the truth is that we shall never reach the past unless we frankly place ourselves within it. Essentially virtual, it cannot be known as something past unless we follow and adopt the movement by which it expands into a present image, thus emerging from obscurity into the light of day.[20]

Bergson supports his claim with the simple observation that it is only one's consciousness of one's own body that determines what is experienced as past and present, and that "from the moment [memory] becomes image, the past leaves the state of pure memory and coincides with a certain part of [the] present."[21] In Bergson's construction, involuntary memory and unconscious gesture, spontaneous "truth-tellings," come closer to true memory, as recollection is always itself a narratization. Such stories never quite touch the past, even as we rely on such narratives for making meaning in the present.

In Culbertson's illustration, what Bergson has articulated as a tension between a moment and one's recollection thereof becomes a struggle between what the body knows and the multiple cultural pressures brought to bear on its speaking, as "What we normally call memory is not the remembered at all of course, but a socially accepted fabrication, a weaving together of the thin, sometimes delicate and intertwined threads of true memory, the re-membered, so that these [stories] might be told. Memory is always in the end subjected to those conventions which define the believable."[22] In its syntax, Culbertson's "re-membered" resonates with Toni Morrison's "rememory," Melvin Dixon's "re-membering," and with Linda Hogan's evocation of phantom pain, which finds extension in Nathaniel Mackey's rendition of the same phenomenon, referring to the phantom limb as "a felt recovery, a felt advance beyond severance and limitation that contends with and questions conventional reality, that is a feeling for what is not there that reaches beyond it as it calls into question what is. . . . The phantom limb haunts or critiques a condition in which feeling, consciousness itself, would seem to have been cut off."[23]

It is here that one must come to wonder if *Kindred* is perhaps more sophisticated than it may at first seem, as Butler's recourse to time travel is so successful in its representation of what might emerge out of the gap between what Bergson describes as memory and what Culbertson reminds to us as the social and historical demands of narrative. It is no accident that Butler makes both Kevin and Dana writers, who both become frustrated with their inability to put pen to paper after they return from their respective journeys to the past. Ironically, their writer's blocks in fact dramatize a readerly crisis, as neither Butler nor her characters can really understand the past as long as it is only a tale, a book. But by writing the tale as a living, as a life in the past experienced as a present taking place in a "real environment of memory," Butler makes history incarnate.[24] By thus using Dana's life as a metaphor for the experience of reading, Butler transmutes what could have been a very "easy" text about traumatic repetition into a book about haunting, insofar as reading may be understood as the best metaphor for haunting, in this instance an experience of coming unto one's own experience of a past that is not proper to one's self, but that nonetheless resonates with something in the self, a transmutation of history into an *experience* of reading, into a memory over which one can now claim ownership, rememory.

Though they are painfully successful readers, Dana and Kevin are, inevitably, failed writers. At the end of *Kindred,* Dana and Kevin travel to Maryland, hoping to uncover what happened to the people whom they had come to know in their time-travel. But the people they seek news of were slaves, and Kevin and Dana cannot learn how their stories ended because such stories were never archived. It is fitting, then, that in the last pages of *Kindred* we are left with an image of Dana and Kevin, scarred, dismembered, and years beyond their proper ages, sitting on the steps of the Maryland Historical Society, commiserating in their knowledge that history has not preserved even for them the world they once knew. It is in this sense that Butler's time-traveling protagonist has perhaps indeed supplied us with an apt metaphor for the experience not of history, but of trauma after all, for it is to the site of an historical damage that Dana travels, the sight of which consolidates and makes speakable the tension between herself and her white husband. *Trapped there, the violation seems to continue in a reverberating present that belies the supposed linearity of time and the possibilities of endings.*

Rather than think of Dana's travel as a literal transportation between separate times and places, consider her travel as instead made possible by the turning of her own body, folding inside out and back again. It is a journey into her own interiority, a place beholden to the facts of her own body's history. This journey, made possible by the genre, is one through which symbols indeed "tend to actualize," as the act of reading becomes an enactment of the text, which for the reader is a book, but for Dana her own body, a body that bespeaks history—think here, even, of how much we are made to understand Dana resembles Alice, Rufus' slave concubine/Dana's distant foremother: this body incarnates history, as the traumatizing elements of Dana's past are made accessible to herself, thus collapsing the boundary between the self as a self and the self as another, collapsing the boundary between now and then. In *Kindred,* this reverberation is literalized through the conventions of science fiction, yet it is in fact best understood as an act of reading taken to the absolute extreme of the reader becoming the text, perhaps in fact realizing that she has been the text all along: an absolute identity.

TRAUMA IS FOR THE LIVING

We must wonder: why Dana? Why must *she* bear the burden of this story? As a protagonist, Dana is a proxy for the author's own experiences of haunting, and enables Butler's otherwise impossible mission—to show how she as reader can never know her ancestors' experiences, but that she can nonetheless represent their stories, not by retelling their stories, but by instead forcing her protagonist to continually encounter the limits of her own knowledge, the archival past she has herself constructed through her consumption of cultural products, mainly film and history texts. It is as if Butler puts Dana in an historically mimetic space, and forces her to encounter the schism between a sense of reality and its representation, between social history and mimesis. *Kindred*, in this sense, is like a trip to Colonial Williamsburg gone terribly wrong, as the barrier between consuming the cultural product and becoming that product deteriorates—the real sign of a successful immersion in history. In this sense, Dana becomes the history that she has consumed, and when thought of this way *Kindred* becomes less explicitly about a woman's travel to a troubled past and more about an individual's experience of reading about his or her own past, or more generally about cultural experiences of places technically inaccessible to us, even as they constitute us. It is our resistance to slipping between is and isn't, self and non-self, that keeps our relationship to the past a mere shade away from an absolutely uncanny modality, that keeps us from over-experiencing history's reverberations, as Dana has.

In *Kindred,* history's reverberations, like experiences of the uncanny, seem generated by visual cues, the apotheosis being the notion that Dana must travel to the past in order to see herself in the present. There is something suspicious about this, which can perhaps help us with this question of "why Dana?" At the novel's core we find a domestic tale. In fact, if one were to take away the tale's more fantastical elements, one would be left with the simple story of a newly married couple, challenged by their ongoing encounter with the wife's familial past. But when subjected to science fiction's capacity for actualization, the story takes on epic proportions, as a personal problem is thematically enlarged, here coming to carry the burden of a sexual relationship's historical reverberations: There is a white man and a black woman, married. One day, the wife finds herself catapulted into the past, where she is forced to live as a slave. Eventually, he too makes the trip, so that their married relationship becomes one of a master and his slave concubine, thus mirroring the historical relationship at the core of her own identity.

Attached to such a tale is a sense of guilt regarding interracial romance, or more specifically, a muted awareness of what loving white men, like wearing red, might invite back to the woman herself. For even despite the hints at recuperation in Kevin and Dana's relationship, it is clear that the facts of history will keep it a tenuous enterprise still beholden to history's reverberations. Indeed, if one were to melt together the reverberations that *Kindred* maps across historical time, one would be left with a single word: *rape*. Butler seldom uses it, but it is always there. Hyperpresent even in its silence, its fact and threat superimposes onto the text another structure of relation that moves across time and space, the contrapuntal rationale to Dana's obligations to life—"No": rape; "I don't feel safe anymore": rape; "not as my master, not as my lover": rape. The fact of sexual violence permeates *Kindred*, much as it pervades the very convoluted imbrications of race and kinship at the backbone of post-encounter civilization in the New World. Whenever Dana appears in the present with the scars and bruises she has sustained in her slave past in Maryland, her friends and family assume she got them from Kevin. You get a sense that they feel sorry for her.

A white man dating a black woman. The couple will always draw black looks, the black gaze: *Don't you know that they raped our women?* The question, which collects and articulates the onlooker's backward gaze (through the woman—who has now become an unspeaking and transparent object gelled in her country's historical legacy of rape and violence), takes away historical wonder's play and enchantment, for who could ever say "yes"? Historical imbrication is one of the social's most difficult ironies (or tortures), and is played out most strikingly in the visual, as the image of Kevin and Dana together channels for some onlookers thoughts of previous crimes and victimizations, of structures of relation that shaped the lives of their ancestors, of people who looked just like Kevin, just like Dana, and just like themselves. Such ghosting is vital, for it is a way of mapping one's way through the forests of misrecognition and uncanny synonymies, and it is this move, from making wounds to feeling and sharing pain, that helps our stumble towards dismantling structures of power, thus helping us reconfigure and re-imagine our relations to each other. As Culbertson notes, "Violence is always and necessarily about wounding—physical harm which is often permanent—even when this is only implied or threatened. Wounding, the penetration of the skin, is the baseline, the reference point, of all violence, and of all power relationships sustained by violence." She goes on to note that

> Clearly, wounding results in pain, and so the two are intimately related; they differ in that pain is only sometimes a result of the eminently social process of wounding, and that wounding always causes some sort of pain, even if, as in the deep wounding of soldiers in the heat of battle, it might not be sensed at the moment. More simply, wounding is, as I use the term, a social act; pain is a state of being, an experience.[25]

During her second travel to Maryland, Dana narrowly escapes being raped by a white patroller. When she first returns to her own home, she, in a frenzy, attacks Kevin, unable to at first recognize him as her white husband and not as the white patroller. Later, worried that she may be taken to the past again, Kevin reveals the anxiety the episode has brought to him: "Do I look like someone you can come home to from where you may be going?"[26] Dana's time travel makes apparent a scar in her and Kevin's relationship, as now they must necessarily experience the pain, even though they did not make the wound. It is an historical wound, and we must wonder if Kevin and Dana's marriage heals or opens it. To paraphrase Culbertson, *wounding is a social act; haunting is an experience.*

Kindred is not a novel that works to revise or counter extant histories, but rather one that works to establish a sense of the already-written, and thus open a category that may rightfully be called the *always*, that which must always, necessarily, be repeated and re-experienced in the name of the future. Most people, from professor to third grader, can espouse the benefits of knowing one's history, most often asserting that we must learn history so that history does not repeat itself. I must admit, though, that I have never quite understood this claim, which I find much akin to the deterrent model of criminal justice. The fact of jail does not prevent most crime; the fact of the Holocaust did not prevent, for instance, ethnic cleansing in Rwanda, just as Argentina's "disappearances" did not prevent disappearances in Guatemala. In other words, there is little evidence that perpetrators learn from history. However, by making Kevin and Dana's relationship a healing force, Butler moves us toward a sense of therapeutic regeneration in interracial love. But this therapy, like the process of coming to identify with one's own history, does not come without risk and comes at considerable cost. Every time Kevin and Dana make love, usually after she has returned from the past, he hurts her even as he heals her, chafing her bruises and reopening her cuts, reminders of the scenes of brutal violence she faced at the hands of white men only moments before. By not disavowing her pain, but at the same time knowing what wounds her (and not doing it), Kevin, in their lovemaking, simultaneously reminds her *of* and also screens her *from* a reiteration of her own possible degradation.

It is this friction between pleasure and pain, between damage and recuperation, that indicates the alternative and potentially transformative space that makes Dana's time travel possible in the first place. In *Kindred*, transgression enables transportation, as history's lesson can only be revealed to those who violate the mandate it has placed on the future. One "only" need "see" history to discover, to remember, why such mandates are necessary, which is why history's lessons are always, only, mere repetition. Meanwhile, Dana's present—love—opens her to the facts of rape and coercion in her past—violence. At this juncture comes the fruition of the recuperative possibilities of learning history, both as an individual awakening and as a pedagogical exercise: Perpetrators don't learn from history, victims do. Don't you know that they raped our women? "Yes." Do I look like someone you could come home to? "Yes."

6 Winding Sheets
Petry and Wright

> . . . to write ghost stories implies that ghosts are real, that is to say, that they produce material effects. To impute a kind of objectivity to ghosts implies that, from a certain standpoint, the dialectics of visibility and invisibility involve a constant negotiation between what can be seen and what is in the shadows.[1]
>
> —Avery Gordon

Underlying Octavia Butler's *Kindred* is a notion of what is at stake in recognizing oneself as culturally produced by forces as powerful as any found in the natural world. In *Kindred* we are given two opposing senses of the cultural's power. On the one hand, exposure to cultural texts—novels, films, and so on—enables Dana's comprehension of herself as an historical subject. When she is catapulted back into the past, she comes armed with at least some knowledge of where she is and what it means for her. At the same time, she also quickly realizes that secondhand knowledge, reading, is insufficient to the task of living in a time and place that she had only previously encountered as a text. It is only because of the extraordinary circumstance of time travel, however, that Butler's protagonist could come to see this difference. Otherwise, she might have likely gone forth in her life like the rest of us, negotiating the balance between what we know through living and what we come to know through our experiences of other people's lives. Despite any nagging feelings, despite any sense that the past's meanings are shading her own life, she would likely live her life without any moment in which the historical forces that have come to shape her would ever quite emerge fully into view.

Every once in a while, however, one encounters a cultural object that brings the presence of such forces into sharp relief. Such is the case with James Baldwin's response to Richard Wright's *Native Son*, a response that has been well-critiqued in the annals of African-American literary scholarship. And *Native Son* is indeed an important text, if only because no text has brought to American readers a more compelling vision of segregation's damage. Combined with its heavy borrowing from Marxist and social scientific discourse, the sense that Wright's book is an essential text, a canonical text, means that readers often likely approach it as an authority regarding the social plight of urban African Americans—or, as my students often say, "It's just so real. Wright just feels so real!"

To see this kind of authority handed over to a text can be grating, especially when set in combination with the novel's popularity. We can hear such an irritation just beneath the surface of Baldwin's famous assertion regarding *Native Son*, that "No American Negro exists who does not have his private Bigger Thomas living in his skull."[2] Baldwin's frustration and resignation are audible in his sarcastic image of a miniaturized, "private Bigger Thomas" and in his choice of "skull," instead of mind or psyche. Skull, bone, attaches Bigger's meaning to Baldwin's material body, an attachment that gestures towards the sonic, towards a sense of being subjected to a bodily vibration over which one does not have control, a pounding headache, or the reverberation from someone else's stereo. Bone: material, structural. Skull, essential, but also a whiff of death and the impersonal, of the body as shell, as that which is inhabited by the self, or, as in Baldwin's case, by another. In Baldwin's irritation we thus hear frustration, as Lawrie Balfour puts it, with living with an identity "hidden in the formulation, 'the Negro . . . '"[3] As we have seen in earlier chapters, and will also explore again later, Baldwin was himself willing to offer up a category, Negro, and to fill it with meaning. His umbrage, however, comes here with the article, with the object status, the formulation. The Negro. Bigger. Nigger.

SINCERE ART

Bigger Thomas, Richard Wright's protagonist in *Native Son*, is indeed a formulation. This is intentional, for he is a character written to explicate the impact of racism on the urban poor and black, an explication informed by Wright's avid interests in sociology, psychology, and criminology.[4] Indeed, in his introduction to Horace Cayton and St. Clair Drake's landmark 1945 anthropological study of African-American life in Chicago, *Black Metropolis*, Wright takes great pains to emphasize how his own work had been influenced by the authors, as well as by the work of The Chicago School of Sociology, which was at the time known specifically for its innovations in the sociology of the urban world. As far as Wright was concerned, each enterprise worked in the service of the other, even going so far as to enjoin the reader to read *Black Metropolis*, if he or she at all doubted the veracity of any claims he made in *Native Son*.[5]

Black Metropolis tells the story of African American migration to Chicago: where people came from, where they ended up, and what they did when they got there. Cayton and Drake also examine how each of these phenomena was determined by the various white legal and social apparatuses that limited African American migration to one segment of the city, the Black Belt. As a formulation, a symbol, Bigger is perfectly aligned with that school of thought's approach to the human, which focuses on the human as coming into being through social and environmental impact, rather than as through heredity. In this analysis, the city is ripe for observation because the space of the city supplies a closed system, a discrete field of examination.

Black Metropolis, with its maps, charts, and extensive historical detail, helped Wright to comprehend and thereby come to terms with a city that had come close to claiming his life. By coming into knowledge of his circumstance and social condition, he was eventually able to rescue himself from his losing battle with Chicago's urban environment, later reflecting that

> there is an open and raw beauty about [Chicago] that seems either to kill or endow one with the spirit of life. I felt those extremes of possibility, death and hope, while I lived half hungry and afraid in a city to which I had fled with the dumb yearning to write, to tell my story. But I did not know what my story was, and it was not until I stumbled upon science that I discovered some of the meanings of the environment that battered and taunted me [. . . .] I found that sincere art and honest science were not far apart, that each could enrich the other. The huge mountains of fact piled up by the Department of Sociology at the University of Chicago gave me my first concrete vision of the forces that molded the urban Negro's body and soul.[6]

In what he stages here as an epic encounter, science awakens in Wright an understanding of the relationship between self and environment. This knowledge frees him from a poverty of both stomach and spirit, as the "huge mountains of fact" give form to an otherwise ghostly torment—in the sense that Wright, the previously anonymous "urban Negro," could previously only feel the effects of the various unnamable forces that shaped his life, forces that could "kill" or "endow" and that are only vaguely referenceable as "the environment." "Dumb," but not deaf, the urban migrant subject can experience but cannot write his own tale, until science enables his authorship.

With *Native Son*, Wright was able to create his own field of examination, a space from which he could bring back the results of his investigation into what it "meant" to be black in Chicago. As Farah Griffin has pointed out, after his acquisition of science such qualities would come to describe the subjects of Wright's writing, and no longer himself:

> To understand the world of Wright's migrants it is necessary to understand the ways in which power functions as domination and exploitation. It functions on them not just as economic subjects but also as racial subjects. These men are poor and black. They are cyclical in a world of linear time. They are often confused and motivated by fear. Most lack an understanding of the forces that act upon them. Only Wright himself claims any enlightenment in this sphere, and with understanding comes further alienation and dissatisfaction.[7]

Without an understanding of the forces that shape them, being in the world means living in response to power's subjection—its determinate narrative regarding the social meaning of their bodies, and also in deference to power's subjugation—its determination of how black bodies move in space, vis-à-vis that meaning. In such a formulation, anything that might be referred to as the self mainly exists as a sum of affective responses, unable to move forward and away from circumstance. Early in his career, such social forces are made comprehensible to Wright through the workings of "honest science" so that he might make them visible to others through art.[8]

We must of course question how successfully Wright in fact balances art and science, particularly as his sense of the scientific draws a great deal of its authority from a primary difference from art. By virtue of this denial he misses an opportunity to mine the potential incommensurability between the language of the analytic that helps him to understand the world, and the languages African Americans have built up in the service of rendering such lives livable. There is always potentially a gap between our analyses of experience and our experiences of living in the world. This incommensurability, which Jean-François Lyotard would refer to as a *differend*, sociologist Avery Gordon characterizes as a foundation for her notion of haunting.[9]

"In haunting," Gordon tells us, "organized forces and systemic structures that appear removed from us make their impact felt in everyday life in a way that confounds our analytic separations and confounds the social separations themselves."[10] For Gordon, this gap created by "the disjuncture between identifying a social structure (or declaring its determinate existence) and its articulation in everyday life and thought," is an ultimately productive space of "vision" and "affliction," from which writers can bring into public discourse certain narratives of effect, but must often, later and alone, face the remainders, the ghostly affects brought to them by their objects of study, who are often parallel to themselves. This space of vision and affliction is not unlike the space inhabited by the alienated artist, the exile and the expatriate. It is the space of the world's Baldwins and Wrights; it is an uncomfortable space in which one is subject to the privileges and dissimulations of a simultaneously insider and outsider status, the "further alienation" Griffin notes above.

According to Gordon, the discomfort experienced in this space where experience haunts analysis is not unlike the discomfort imagination brings to sociological inquiry. She argues that that which the literary has license to enlarge, "the fictive," often threatens to explode the authority of "the sociological," and it is for this reason that the sociological is always vexed, if not hexed, by the fictive:

> By the fictive I mean not simply literature but . . . the ensemble of cultural imaginings, affective experiences, animated objects, marginal voices, narrative densities, and eccentric traces of power's presence. For sociology, the fictive is our constitutive horizon of error; it is what

> has been and must be exiled to ordain the authority of the discipline and the truthful knowledge sociology can claim to produce.[11]

The power that *Native Son* has over many of its readers, which plays out as a sense that the novel speaks the truth about a certain kind of existence, is ultimately grounded in its authority, an authority grounded in the kinds of discourses, referenceable languages, in which it is written. The simultaneously present and illusory fictive, meanwhile, resides at a distance from the authority of referenceable and reproducible knowledge. Art, in this sense, is that which science must be moved away from.[12] In *Black Metropolis*, as well as in "How Bigger Was Born," Wright would assert that men like Bigger, by virtue of their living conditions, only intellectually and emotionally develop in the most basic ways. Such reduction in personhood is inevitable because "The imposed conditions under which Negroes live detail the structure of their lives like an engineer outlining the blue-prints for the production of machines."[13] This clues us into how the possibility of Wright's scientific understanding of Bigger Thomas' condition turns on a metaphor antithetical to Bigger's humanity: Bigger is a machine. But, when Wright tries to set this machine in motion, to make it dance so that we may understand its workings, Wright is faced with a real problem: his protagonist, whose destiny it is to destroy, does not necessarily want to kill, even as he must, if the larger meaning of the narrative is ever to come into being vis-à-vis the meaning-potential of his environment.

BLACK METROPOLIS

Chicago, a favored destination for people in search of new or better lives, emblematized for more than a century the paradoxical nature of urban migration. The city promised a newness sited in the modern metropolis, even as, despite the optimism of its arrivistes, the city was and is also an exemplar of the tension between the utopian hope of transformation through planning and policy, and the dystopia of cultural and economic entrapment. Unlike many older cities to its east, with their hodge-podge of neighborhoods, vaguely separated by alleys and squares, Chicago is built onto a rigid grid, thus the "long, straight streets" Wright references in "How Bigger Was Born." Living in Chicago it is easy to believe that its neighborhoods could never even tentatively tumble into one another, and that concomitantly, the inhabitants of its various neighborhoods are where they live, which is to say that the city is easily experienced as continuous with its citizenry. This may be a way of thinking about why Wright claims that the city's homes hold an "old destiny," for in Chicago it often seems that things are as they are because they reflect a natural order, a social organicism rooted in the deep is-ness of the world's absolute differences, raw, stark, and brutal.[14] Perhaps this is why, despite the impact of the 1871 fire on the city's geography, again, the long, straight streets, the city's racial segregation finds its historical fulcrum at the 1919 riot, the other Great Fire. The summer riot, which began as a dispute between black and white on one of Chicago's segregated beaches and soon spilled out into the city, consolidated the "Black Belt"—then a long, narrow tract of black neighborhoods on the South Side of Chicago—into a separate "black metropolis."

By justifying the city's already strained race-relations, this final split between its North-, South-, and West-sides set the stage for Chicago's ascension as one of the nation's most segregated cities. Undergirding all other kinds of difference, spatial boundaries would thus emerge as both the primary tool and representation of social difference in Chicago.[15] After the 1919 riot, increased hatred between the races, coupled with the almost total economic shutdown the area suffered as a result of white businesses refusing to open during the riot, prompted the Belt to close in on itself, to become a city within a city, a fortified structure whose boundaries were vehemently secured from the outside. *Native Son*, like *Black Metropolis*, is staked on a notion that, even as white power touches black lives in a variety of ways, in Chicago that power's most nefarious workings are expressed spatially. In *Black Metropolis*, Cayton and Drake are careful to report that even as Chicago had always been a city of migrants, particularly from eastern and southern Europe, blacks could not as easily attain the geographical mobility that usually comes with economic success. Unlike other groups, African Americans were not eventually absorbed into the larger population, even as they increased in class status.[16] In this way, space came to make race, as spatial deployment makes race intelligible, giving it meaning and recognizability. This knot, according to Cayton and Drake, cannot be untangled, as the racialized subject occupies the physical *and* psychic space of the abject.

It is difficult not to fall into the determinism ourselves. But as Henri Lefebvre reminds us in *The Production of Space*, not only do spatializations come to inhabit us, but we also of course inhabit space. The meanings of such simultaneity are powerful, for we must also consider the following:

> . . . there is an immediate relationship between the body and its space, between the body's deployment in space and its occupation of space. . . . each living body is space and has its space: it produces itself in space and also produces that space. This is truly a remarkable relationship: the body with the energies at its disposal, the living body, creates or produces its own space; conversely, the laws of space, which is to say the laws of discrimination in space, also govern the living body and the deployment of its energies.

Not only are our experiences of space duplicated as psychic experiences, but also we produce the meaning of space through our presences. Note, however, how Lefebvre is careful to ground this reciprocity in law, in the rules that determine how our bodies are allowed to occupy space. In our experiences of space we also experience law, as both formal and informal restriction, and with all its attendant moral and ethical meanings. It is unsurprising, then, that we may find in spatiality a correlate to our existences in the social world.

As Victor Burgin points out, the language we use to talk about our experiences of spatiality nonetheless reflects a process of naturalization so complete that it can approach the language of psychosis, namely clinical paranoia, insofar as deep attachments to segregation, for instance, require a process not unlike that by which a psychotic is able to project onto "some larger screen," for instance "the 'body politic' of nation, or race," a threat originally perceived as being against his or her own body.[17] To get at this, Burgin offers the following example, derived from a 1989 *New York Times* article:

> Two communities in the town of Malverne, New York: one mostly Black, the other mainly White. The reporter writes, "The two are divided by Ocean Avenue, and residents on both sides refer to the other as 'over the ocean.'" In this example, and in the extreme case, the clinically paranoid person would quite simply *see* an ocean, in a less marked paranoid attitude the subject would behave exactly *as if* there were an ocean—with all the absolute territorial imperatives, all the patriotic moral fervor attached to the defense of the motherland, that this could invoke.[18]

Not only do spatial metaphors allow us to articulate social differences as spatial distances, they serve to legitimize the enforcement of difference, the behaving "exactly *as if*."

When we set Burgin's understanding against Lefebvre's notion of reciprocity, we can come to a working definition of segregation as a manifestation of abstract or political space that is bolstered by the deployment of bodies in a concrete geography, a deployment that is itself motivated and reinforced by the language we use to describe, to map, that geography. Even as a map of Chicago would, for instance, symbolize on its surface the city's spatial organization, on the B-side of such a map we would find other kinds of inscriptions, traces of what the map's surface cannot so easily represent—racial deployments, terrible bombings, the tension of communities adjacent but seldom touching. Further, these other spatial realities, unsymbolized, are as well mapped in the psyche of Wright's Chicagoan protagonist, Bigger Thomas. Segregation is thus a word for the conscious and unconscious regulation of a lived space that reflects, enacts, and upholds the abstraction. The purpose of segregated space is to make us forget that social separations, particularly racial and class ones, are artificial and require continuous enforcement, that they too have a history. Such space, is, by necessity, amnesiac space, and this amnesia is kept active via a logic of difference, in the sense that segregation produces difference by making it apparent, even as the mechanism by which this happens is itself transparent: visible, but not quite real, segregation makes racial relationships apparitional. This is not unlike the mechanism of what Jacques Lacan refers to as "delusional metaphor," which results from the exchange of a signifier for the signified, a Symbol for the Thing.[19] We might call this world a ghost world, though we of course also know how the idea of a thing, its shadow, can at times hurt more than the material thing itself.

Today there is still a Black Belt, though, as it has expanded exponentially to the south and to the west, it is now simply known as the South Side of Chicago. And although small parts of the city are indeed less segregated, whenever I return to *Native Son* I find that Bigger's sense of boundaries—his sense of streets that divide neighborhoods as if they were warring nations, the fear he feels when behind enemy lines and his ambiguous relief upon returning to the confines of his own territory—this knowledge is still in evidence. Even today, my grandmother still warns: *Make sure your tank is filled when you drive to the airport; you don't want to stop at night in Marquette Park*. Or I watch my mother refuse to get gas in Bridgeport, two blocks from her house, *because it's really just not safe*, if you know what I mean. This is the underside of Lefebvre's assertion that the body "produces itself in space and also produces that space," and also gets at why we care so much about space—why segregation hurts and how it so deeply damages. It hurts because its restrictions require one to bring into oneself the specular visage (because you have to see it not to have it) of what one must be kept from if one is to be a properly oppressed subject. When we talk about space we must necessarily talk about the self, for the psyche is the site of space's reverberations, as our experiences of space build up an interior topos that structures our relationship to the world.[20] It is by virtue of such reverberation that there is no sense of space without subjectivity, and, more importantly, no subjectivity without an orientation in space.

In *Native Son*, every body is brought into relation with a spatialized meaning. It is important to remember, however, that the power of reinforcement in the 1940s absolutely rested in white bodies, in lines drawn by white hands imagining themselves working for the protection of white bodies. As Wright describes it in *Native Son*, being so imbued with this power gives white bodies a power far in excess of any notion of the human:

> To Bigger and his kind white people were not really people; they were a sort of great natural force. . . . As long as he and his black folks did not go beyond certain limits, there was no need to fear that white force. But whether they feared it or not, each and every day of their lives they lived with it; even when words did not sound its name, they acknowledged its reality. As long as they lived here in this prescribed corner of the city, they paid mute tribute to it.[21]

Despite his "mute tribute" to them, it is important to note that there are indeed moments during *Native Son* when Bigger is emotionally articulate about how these forces affect him. In such moments, it seems less that Bigger is incapable of comprehending his relationship to the social forces that shape him than that he knows that, in order to live, he must live *as if* he does not know. Rather than of living without consciousness, it is a matter, then, of repressing the emergence thereof, if he is to live in his prescribed place in the city.

GHOST IN THE MACHINE

In my discussion of *Kindred* in the previous chapter, I reference some of Roberta Culbertson's work on the relationship between space, trauma, and signification. In that chapter, Culbertson is useful towards a consideration of how the body might bear knowledge in excess of what the conscious self allows itself to remember, which also sets the conditions for the mind being haunted *by* the body. She notes that in addition to experiences of temporal disruption regularly associated with consciousness in the wake of a traumatic experience, for instance repetitions and flashbacks, a memory of trauma might also be experienced as "the memory of other levels of reality, sensed not even by the five senses, *but by the body itself, or by the spiritual mind, the interior of the body*"—as a transportation to another place.[22] Culbertson goes on to add that without access to language, or perhaps even to image—without access to any level of representation at risk of touching consciousness—such memories are particularly vulnerable to being misrecognized as approaching the self from outside of the self or as experiences of the self *as* outside of the self—as haunting or as an out-of-body experience—as materializations of what would otherwise only be understood as word, as symbol. Thus, "When such gross tools as language are brought to bear on the experience, the result appears to be metaphor, but it is not. As Terrence Des Pres says, in circumstances of extremity, "symbols tend to actualize."

Bigger is fully occupied by the restrictions put on him as an African American, as his material world constantly reminds him of what he cannot have and thus becomes an index of what is already lost to him, what is foreclosed to him. So when Bigger and his friend Gus look into the sky and see an airplane, for instance, they see something they cannot have—access to flight lessons, physical and social mobility, somewhere to go—things they cannot have because they are not white.[23] As Houston Baker points out, as a narrative device the plane indeed "signifies what might be called a traditional dynamic of Afro-American place. The transport and the skywriter suggest the narrow confinement of black life; they point to a dreadful dichotomy between black and white experience in the New World."[24] But it is also important to imagine that, for Bigger and Gus, the plane is not a metaphor, for it is *exactly* what they both consciously and unconsciously know they cannot have. It is what it is: an airplane.

Looking at the airplane, Bigger has a flash of insight, declaring to Gus that "they," the white folks, "don't let us do nothing." This insight, prompted by the plane and articulated in spatial terms, is actualized, experienced, as a physical violation:

> I know I oughtn't think about it, but I can't help it. Every time I think about it I feel like somebody's poking a red-hot iron down my throat. Goddammit, look! We live here and they live there. We black and they white. They got things and we ain't. They do things and we can't. It's just like living in jail. Half the time I feel like I'm on the outside of the world peeping in through a knot-hole in the fence. . . . [25]

The swear, "Goddammit," is Bigger's most articulate line in the novel, as its injunction, "look!" makes both racial and spatial claims, in the sense that it requires the reader to recognize through Bigger previously transparent mechanisms of difference, a consciousness Bigger himself comes to through his recognition of contrast: here/there, black/white, got/ain't got, contrasts that to him represent the inside and outside of the world, and also the world's simultaneous restriction and violation of his body. Wright's recourse to the corporeal frames Bigger's sense of his place in the city as inextricable from his sense of his self in his own body: "every time I think about it I feel like somebody's poking a red-hot iron down my throat." The following conversation ensues:

> 'Gus?'
> 'Hunh?'
> 'You know where the white folks live?'
> 'Yeah,' Gus said, pointing eastward. 'Over across the "line"; over there on Cottage Grove Avenue.'
> 'Naw; they don't,' Bigger said.
> 'What you mean?' Gus asked, puzzled. 'Then, where do they live?'
> Bigger doubled his fist and struck his solar plexus.
> 'Right down here in my stomach,' he said.
> Gus looked at Bigger searchingly, then away, as though ashamed.
> 'Yeah; I know what you mean,' he whispered.
> 'Every time I think of 'em, I feel 'em,' Bigger said.
> 'Yeah; and in your chest and throat, too,' Gus said.
> 'It's like fire.'
> 'And sometimes you can't hardly breathe. . . . '[26]

As Gus points to the geographical source of their pain, to the white folks who live "over across the 'line,'" Bigger's act of marking that source immediately turns to himself, to the site of that pain. When he strikes himself, he thus substitutes the experienced pain of his social condition for his own realization of that pain's source. Fire—*Fy-ah Lawd!*—symbol and Thing, simultaneously referencing both the understanding and the pain: the bombs, the violence, the loss inherent to his place in the world. Riots, my grandfather once told me, never destroy white neighborhoods. Under segregation, enforced distance guarantees the incorporation of a disciplinary presence as the whitefolk inhabit, and according to Wright, motivate, Bigger.

It is important to notice that when Bigger asks Gus to locate the white folks, Gus' answer comes easily as he points to a specific location. Inherent in his response is a recognition of the geographical boundary that makes his and Bigger's localized sense of racial difference possible, "the line." The Daltons, whose house is at 4605 Drexel Blvd., live adjacent to this line, Drexel being the wide boulevard that at the time separated white Hyde Park from the Black Belt, marked by Cottage Grove immediately to the west and to its north by Bronzeville, a neighborhood that was at the time slowly becoming a part of the Black Belt. The Daltons' inhabitation of a geographically liminal space is mirrored in the life choices of the house's inhabitants as well, in Mary's socialite Communism and in the Daltons' slum-lord philanthropy. When Mary and Jan refuse to maintain the boundaries that make possible the world they and Bigger inhabit, they bring crisis by suggesting to Bigger that he forget the very segregation that, according to Wright, founded his subjectivity.

Later that night, alone with Mary in her room, Bigger is faced with the possibility that Mary and Jan had told the truth, that he could cross the boundary between black and white. Almost immediately, however, Mrs. Dalton, a "white blur," appears, "hovering" like a ghost.[27] As he looks at her, the boundary between his interiorized understanding of the world and the reality of the moment disintegrates, for her appearance at once prophesies to and reminds Bigger of the cultural meaning of his appearance in this space haunted by a deadly racial history. She is the prompt, and Bigger experiences a rememory. He has stepped into that other world, a world that was already there, waiting for him:

> He clenched his teeth and held his breath, intimidated to the core by the awesome white blur floating toward him. His muscles flexed taut as steel and he pressed the pillow, feeling the bed give slowly, evenly, but silently. Then suddenly her fingernails did not bite into his wrists. Mary's fingers loosened. He did not feel her surging and heaving against him. Her body was still.[28]

When Bigger realizes what he has done, "The reality of the room fell from him" as "the vast city of white people that sprawled outside took its place."[29] When he kills, whites take up their proper place outside of his body. Thus exorcised, Bigger comes into narrative and into, according to Wright, Being: "What I killed for I *am*! It must've been pretty deep in me to make me kill! I must have felt it awful hard to murder. . . ."[30] Indeed.

To say that Mrs. Dalton is a ghost is not to say that she isn't real, flesh and blood, even as to say that she is real does not disentangle her from Bigger's imagination; it in fact makes her more than real. When Bigger kills Mary, he is brought into agency through an accidental event, one that he immediately responds to as an intentional event, thus assigning to it a criminal meaning that is in fact a priori to his own act, and that he retroactively applies to his own understanding of how Mary Dalton died (this is evidenced in his inability to properly name his own crime, for instance when he later claims that he did rape her, and thus steps into his prescheduled narrative). When Mrs. Dalton comes into Mary's room, Bigger sees himself mirrored in her blind eyes—not as who he is, merely a black man in the wrong place at the wrong time, but as who he should be vis-à-vis the dominant narrative of what it means to be a black man in that space. His fear is based on his correct understanding that there is already a larger cultural meaning attached to his presence in Mary's room, a meaning that no amount of explanation could ever account for; his word could never overpower the fact that this room has always been waiting for him, waiting for any black man to become the man he had always been described as being.

WINDING SHEETS AND NATIVE DAUGHTERS

In a short story titled "Like a Winding Sheet," Ann Petry, another African American writer familiar with Communism and writing in the 1940s, offers up an example of how haunting might move into possession, thereby setting the conditions for its own emergence as the inheritance of the possessed subject. The story's short plot maps the degradation of a man named Johnson as he descends into violence, seized by a haunting that turns into him, transforming him from one kind of man to another.

We only hear Johnson's name once in Petry's story, when his forelady calls out to him, berating him for coming to work late.[31] Coming from his boss's mouth, the sound of his name jars the reader, both because the protagonist has gone without a proper name for the first third of the story, and also because we know that he is tired and in pain—he cannot keep up with the nightshift's demanding reversals, and his legs have been damaged by the specific demands of his workplace, where he must walk constantly through the night.[32] The reader also knows that Johnson, this everyman who works nights in a factory, is a good man. Until the forelady calls his name, Petry has built a careful sense that Johnson is a man who works hard and loves his wife, unwilling to "talk to her roughly or to strike her like a lot of men might have done." He, as Petry puts it, "was not made that way." Describing him as "not made that way" conveys more than the sense that he would never hit his wife; it suggests that this is something important that we must know about him, if we are to know him at all. A vision of mid-century black masculinity, restraint is built into Johnson's very constitution: he is above this kind of anger, this kind of response, even when he sees Mae's declaration that she does not want to work on Friday the Thirteenth as kooky and irrational, and knows that arguing with her rather than snapping *on* her, will make him late for work, again. "Aw, come on," he tells her, "Today's payday. And payday is a good luck day everywhere, any way you look at it."

Building on stereotype, Petry also gives us a sense that Johnson is the more practical one in the marriage, while Mae, giggly, lives more effortlessly. She is also superstitious, wanting to refuse to work that day despite it being payday. Petry's stereotypes are also playful: at the beginning of the story Mae, dressed in overalls, jokes to her husband that, laying there in bed, wrapped in a sheet, he looks "like a huckleberry—in a winding sheet." It is a sweet image, a quick sexy image of a lover, vulnerable and familiar, dark and ripe against the white sheets. And it is unfortunate that readers do not get to spend more time with them as they were, content and well into their marriage. Much like *Native Son,* "Like a Winding Sheet" is a story about things that have already happened. Johnson is already dead.

The reader is never given a clear picture of what Johnson and Mae do for a living; we only know that they work in factories and that they work at night. We can glean that Johnson's job entails walking back and forth along the factory floor, gathering assembled pieces of things. Indeed, his labor does not in fact produce anything; it only collects the labor of others. This, however, does not bother him as much as it bothers him that he is never allowed to sit down at work, and that the loud whir and grind of machinery makes human relations at work difficult. He cannot hear the conversations his co-workers have with each other; he can only see their lips moving as he walks from station to station. Only instrumental, without domain or interaction, Johnson is doubly alienated—treated like a machine in his duties and removed from the social systems that would help make such treatment more bearable.

The only human interaction we witness at work is Johnson's encounter with his white forelady. Angry at him for being late, she calls him nigger, by accident:

> He stood motionless for a moment and then turned away from the red lipstick on her mouth that made him remember that the forelady was a woman. He felt a curious tingling in his fingers and he looked down at his hands. They were clenched tight, hard, ready to smash some of the small purple veins in her face.

Unlike his conflict earlier in the day with Mae, it is made clear here that Johnson *would* actually like to hit the forelady. However, refusing to hit a woman is a matter of honor, the assumption being that it is fundamentally unfair for a man to hit a woman because she could never return the blow in kind. Honor is tied to controlling the excess one carries in a relationship; it forces equivalence-making in exchanges in which there would otherwise not be opportunity for equivalence. Johnson would not hit a woman because there is no possibility for such a blow to be a just blow. It is in this way that honor makes justice possible, if only in the sense that it comes into being *as* doing justice to another, an act that is then reflected back as being a characteristic of the self: we say, *he is an honorable man*. The approbation, *he is an honorable man*, satisfies the deferred excess by replacing it with a social value. The very fact of honor's displacements and replacements, however, should also remind us that honor is an illusion, a self-avowedly ethical illusion, but an illusion nonetheless. But, in Petry's story, the illusion's surface—Johnson's honor vis-à-vis gender—is first troubled by class asymmetry: he works for a woman, and is almost broken by a racial asymmetry: the forelady's casual "Nigger." Not only is it a slur, but if the forelady thinks he is a nigger, there never was in fact any possibility for his honor, because a nigger could never appear in this equation as honorable.

On the level of the social, the reader is of course supposed to read Johnson's refusal of violence as *absolutely* honorable, for it is honor in the face of its negation, in the face of challenge. But in the event of the "nigger," there is no possibility for justice because there is no possibility for the future: to call someone a nigger is also a way of declaring that that person will never be anything but a nigger, which is to say that he or she has no possibility outside what he or she has always been, and thus is always and already. When the forelady says "nigger," it *is* a slip, but not in the way she means it. It is not a slip because she did not mean it; it is a slip because she knows that she should not say it to his face. Even she knows the word's power, and fears conjuring the nigger out of Johnson's respectability. And she has been successful, though her escape from the trick is only made possible by Johnson's tethering of *her* nigger to himself, a monumental restraint.

Indeed, Johnson *knows* that he would feel better if he had hit her, declaring that, if he had, the forelady would "never slip and call someone a nigger ever again." But, in lieu of a material retribution that Petry has here made analogous to an exorcism, Johnson instead tries to offer as a sacrifice to his throbbing hands the image of an alternative present-reality:

> He tried to make his hands relax by offering them a description of what it would have been like to strike her because he had the queer feeling that his hands were not exactly a part of him any more—they had developed a separate life of their own over which he had no control. So he dwelt on the pleasure his hands would have felt. . . .

Johnson resists violence, but much as with the pain in his legs, the tension in his hands remains, even after he is "able to think about what had happened without getting upset about it." The excess, big, unreleased, and violent, leaves him shaking and shaken.

The following morning, after standing in line for a cup of hot coffee on his way home from work, Johnson gets to the front to find the urn empty. It is a coincidence, but he does not realize it. Waiting for the coffee to brew, the shopgirl reaches up, innocently, to move her blond hair from her neck, a gesture Johnson misreads as indicating her contempt for him. His misreading is an effect of his prior encounter with the forelady, further revealing how her nigger has cast its shadow over his existence. As he looks at the shopgirl, he realizes that

> what he wanted to do was hit her so hard that the scarlet lipstick on her mouth would smear and spread out over her nose, her chin, out toward her cheeks; so hard that she would never toss her head again and refuse a man a cup of coffee because he was black.

I am reminded here of Ukawsaw Gronniosaw's narrative of his time as a slave, when, after he sees his master reading from the Bible, he cannot understand why the book will not speak to him as it seemingly spoke to his master. Gronniosaw tells us that "this thought immediately presented itself to me, that every body and every thing despis'd me because I was black."[33] Even though the moment is narrated as a flash of insight, its sudden and rather disjointed appearance in the text might also be read as an index of something else, some other event that has gone unnamed, as the reverberation of some other moment that has cast its long shadow over the protagonist's future interpretations of any present moment. There is a similar disconnect in Johnson's assessment of his situation, for not only does he misrecognize the salesgirl's refusal as racism, but his fantasy of retribution singles out the sign of her femininity, her lipstick, rather than the sign of her status as an oppressor, her white skin. Difference, then, is simultaneously misplaced in its move from boss to fellow worker, and displaced in its move from race to gender—as it is moved onto precisely the site through which his honor had formerly come into being.

As in the episode with the forelady, he refrains, and his hands grow more restless. Later that morning, after their long night working, Mae lifts her hair from her neck, and Johnson, still vibrating from the night's injustices "winced away from the gesture." He chastises her for "fooling with her hair," and they almost argue, for she is tired too; she too has worked all night long. But he pulls back, and they make it through the moment. Jokingly, Mae calls him an "old hungry nigger," and the "nigger," a powerful conjure, triggers his hands. The hands smash into Mae's face, exactly replicating his earlier fantasies of retribution against whiteness. He hits her "so hard that the dark red lipstick had blurred and spread over her full lips, reaching up toward the tip of her nose, down toward her chin, out toward her cheeks." Thus possessed, the Johnson we would have liked to have known is dead, and the effects of this social death will reverberate, harming everyone in his life, spiritually and physically haunted by the nigger.

Even as Petry's description of Mae's beating reproduces the description of the earlier violences imagined by Johnson, the status of this event as occurring in the real is represented in a small difference, which is the reference to Mae's "full lips" and her "dark lipstick," lips that signify her blackness, and lipstick that echoes Mae's description of her husband as a huckleberry at the beginning of the story, though now clearly evacuated of the backwater innocence that the term "huckleberry" is slang for:

> The knowledge that he had struck her seeped through him slowly and he was appalled, but he couldn't drag his hands away from her face. He kept striking her and he thought with horror that something inside of him was holding him, binding him to this act, wrapping and twisting about him so that he had to continue it.[34]

With this act, never hitting a woman becomes never hitting a white woman, just as Bigger never would have intentionally harmed Mary Dalton. But Mae or Bigger's girlfriend Bessie? They are always at risk, for they are wound up in the same violence; Mae in the sheet that was once the sign of their companionship, and Bessie, her body cold on an examiner's table, with only the thinnest of sheets between her naked body and the courtroom lights, her body brought to Bigger's trial as the evidence of what Bigger may have done, would have, could have, or should have done to Mary Dalton's body. Much as Mae is made to bear the burden of that which has gone unspoken, Bessie is made to bear the burden of that which has been misspoken, and both suffer the double indignity of having been brought into false equivalence. *In circumstances of extremity, symbols tend to actualize.*

In *Native Son*, Mrs. Dalton's haunting of Bigger jeopardizes the authority of his climatic self-realization, "What I killed for I am!" For by using the figure of Mrs. Dalton to return Bigger's consciousness to him from the outside, Wright misleads the reader into identifying Bigger as the subject rather than as the object of insight. This puts the reader in a voyeuristic relationship to the text, insofar as Wright offers the reader a quiet insider status: we know more about Bigger than he knows about himself, but we are not aware of our edge over him—it is transparent to us—and we are therefore left free to desire more.

And indeed, whether I admit it or not, I always experience a pleasure in reading *Native Son*. This pleasure comes from a sense that Wright has put me on the inside of knowing. So real. But I also know that I hate reading *Native Son*, for not only must I live with this nagging feeling that passage into this inside place has come at the cost of my own body, but also the experience of being doubled as reader and text makes me profoundly uncomfortable. I grew up on the South Side of Chicago, the locus of Wright's socio-artistic heuristic, and Bessie is my grandmother's name. I do not tell you these things so that you might imagine that that is the whole key to my discomfort—except that it kind of is, for they are the kinds of things that nag, yet cannot be included in my analysis because they are too easily mine and thus inadmissible. This knowing first came to me as a teenager, for the first time reading the scene of Bessie's body being brought to Bigger's trial, her suffering forgotten except to elicit the horror of someone else's death. I remember feeling like something was wrong, but that what bothered me was not, as it were, on the table. The feeling later came to me again, in college reading a scene from Wright's *The Color Curtain*. It is the scene in which he recounts an episode in which a white colleague of his at The Bandung Conference worriedly asks him to explain to her the strange ritual her African American roommate is performing, crouched over a fire in a dark corner of their hotel room. Amused and to the rescue, Wright explains that she is furtively straightening her hair.

While trying to explain to his lawyer why he hated Mary Dalton, why he cannot regret killing her, even though he did not mean to, Bigger, "caught in a net of vague, associative memory," recalls a time when his little sister flung her shoe at him because he had "shamed her by looking at her."[35] As I reach for the shoe, it hits me.

Coda
Future Expectations

Blacker than the nighttime sky of Bed-Stuy in July
Blacker than the seed in the blackberry pie
Blacker than the middle of my eye
Black like Fela man cry
Some man wan ask "Who am I?"
I simply reply, "The U.N.I.,
V.E.R.S.A.L. Magnetic"
[. . .]
You're full of big chat but you nah know me
I'm dark like the side of the moon you don't see
when the moon shine newly[1]

—Black Star, "Astronomy (8th Light)"

> Some things had happened to me because I was black, and some things had happened to me because I was me, and I had to discover the demarcation line, if there was one. It seemed that such a demarcation line must certainly exist, but it was also beginning to be borne in on me that it was certainly not easy to find: and perhaps, indeed, when found, not to be trusted . . . Being black affected one's life span, insurance rates, blood pressure, lovers, children, every dangerous hour of every dangerous day.[2]
>
> —Baldwin, "Every Good-Bye Ain't Gone"

A few days after four New York City police officers shot and killed Amadou Diallo in 1999, *New York Times* columnist Clyde Haberman wrote an op-ed piece in which he questioned why so many minorities could characterize some of the violent deaths wrought by the NYPD over the previous few years as examples of "police brutality," much less "murders" or "massacres." Haberman's article touched on several critical issues regarding history, memory, and representation, all of which, for him, boiled down to a matter of evidence. And indeed, in order to recall the series of recent police "mistakes" to his reader, he cited each case (Louima, Diallo, Cedeno, Garcia) as an individual history, each with its own complete narrative of trial and judgment. The fact of acquittal or retraction in each case—the fact of judgment having been passed—to him validated each case as a synchronic event, isolated in history and not part of a larger signifying chain: "While the anger is understandable," Haberman concluded, "it is unclear how anyone can reach such damning conclusions based on the available evidence."[3]

Haberman's conclusions were based on a specific understanding of evidence, where we find it and what counts as such. Furthermore, in his reliance on a sense of history as a record of trials and verdicts, he ultimately used his sense of synchronic history to invalidate the memory of minority communities, communities that, though often silenced in public discourse, nonetheless always remember historical injustice. In other words, where Haberman saw a series of discrete events, predictable consequences of life in a big city, those who through such events have come to understand themselves as similarly at risk see an ongoing pattern of oppression, witness a systemic terror that haunts their daily lives. Such perspectives are seldom understood as being real or reasonable, and are thus not allowed to historicize other events. This means, then, that whereas a person relying on archival knowledge would find a string of isolated events, validated as such by the law, perhaps the victims of such events may see buried inside that history an extended narrative of trials adjudicated without proper witnesses. In other words, what Haberman misses is that memory makes its own judgments. Or as Theodor Adorno once put it, that an "abundance of real suffering tolerates no forgetting." This is important, for without memory's mitigations, history's determinate function can oppress the living and quite capably kill the dead.

RECEPTION OF THE NEWS

In *Passed On: African American Mourning Stories*, Karla Holloway observes the following about black American culture:

> The anticipation of death and dying figured into the experiences of black folk so persistently, given how much more omnipresent death was for them than for other Americans, that lamentation and mortification both found their way into public and private representations of African America to an astonishing degree. [. . . .] Sometimes it was a subtext, but even then the ghostly presence of those narratives reminded us that something about America was, for black folk, disjointed. Instead of death and dying being unusual, untoward events . . . the cycles of our daily lives were so persistently interrupted by specters of death that we worked this experience into the culture's iconography and included it as an aspect of black cultural sensibility . . . [4]

Holloway's notion of the "passed on" simultaneously marks loss and its dissemination, a sense that we are not only threatened by our own impending deaths, but that such threats become haunts by virtue of our experiences—our reception of the news—of other people's deaths. She links this ghosting to a larger sense of life being "disjointed," which attempts to articulate a sense of something being not right, or off. According to Holloway, we can identify a "black cultural sensibility" based in the notion that "the formative years, the waning years, and each day between were haunted by one spiritual's refrain: 'soon one morning, death will come a-calling.'" Holloway's sense of the centrality of death and dying in African-American life can be read as a story about haunting, as an argument for how our experiences of other people's tragedies become continuous with our own livelihoods.[5]

An example: It is late one night, and I have crashed in front of the TV. Disinterested, I settle on the *Essence* awards. The *Essence* show is a yearly event, designed to recognize the contributions of African-American women, mainly celebrities, but also writers, doctors, community workers, and so on. Also, much like the *NAACP Image Awards* and the BET and *Source* awards shows, the *Essence* show is specifically marketed as a black alternative to mainstream, i.e. "white," events. And like any awards show, this night's show featured the usual song and dance: fancy dresses, lots of applause, extended thanks to God and Race. About halfway through the show, there was an extended tribute to the Notorious B.I.G. and Tupac Shakur. Both men had been killed in recent years, and such tributes had become pro-forma and commonplace at the end of the twentieth century. This show, however, soon began to feel different, as its attention seamlessly turned from remembering pop-culture icons to memorializing a long series of African Americans who had been killed in the past year, particularly children who had died in crossfire on city streets. Pictures were shown and mothers were named. Flowers were given. A choir, as if conjured, rang out above the proceedings. To be honest, I found it all quite moving, but then, as suddenly as it had appeared, the awards show that had become a funeral cut to commercial, and when it returned, it was business as usual. Yes, it was a spectacle, but it was really, also, a memorial service.

Over the next few weeks, I would mention the show to friends, just to note how unexpectedly affecting it had been. One day, someone asked me if I hadn't been weirded-out by the fact that I had essentially watched a funeral take place in the middle of the *Essence* awards. Nonplussed, I brushed her off as I had others asking similar questions. *Of course not.* Indeed, whenever telling my story during that long week, I had never felt it necessary to question the event, even as my interlocutors questioned the very veracity of my story. *They really named names? They really brought the families on stage?* Had they missed other recent awards shows, for instance the one when Bone, Thugs-n-Harmony performed "Tha Crossroads," during which the Angel of Death led selected audience members to Heaven? Or other years' shows, like the one when Snoop Dogg staged his own funeral, only to rise from his coffin and perform "Murder Was The

Case" from a wheelchair? Suddenly, as if I were having an out-of-body experience, I watched myself blurt out in frustration, "Funeral, yeah, but whatever: that's just the black part . . ." But then of course I realized, the black part *was* the point, and what does it mean that the "black part," the part that I felt could be explained simply by referring to it *as* black, was not only the culturally different part, but also the beautiful part, the mourning part, the sad part? By representing a series of local deaths in a single funeral, the *Essence* event wove the meaning of those deaths into a larger signifying chain.

In speaking of a population generally familiar with the facts of living too hard and dying too soon, there is nothing new in saying that narratives of mourning and loss are foundational to African-American subjectivity and, by extension, black cultural expression. Perhaps such reaping is inevitable. But accepting this claim also requires an accounting of why many African Americans, who have themselves *not* experienced such lives, nonetheless understand themselves as similarly constituted. You see, the episode of cultural difference that I have described above is not important to me as an illustration of racial difference *as* difference. It is important to me because the appearance of the funeral at the awards show, itself an average and annual commercial venture, served a particular cultural function: to remind me and others like me that such losses are not to be forgotten. They are to be passed on, and to accept this cultural imperative, which is also a political imperative to remember events that are not my own and to testify to their otherwise unwitnessed effects, is to choose to be haunted. In so choosing, the "me" who has been targeted as the show's proper audience is also revealed as constitutive.

Again, I have chosen an example from popular culture in order to highlight the mundanity of the kind of cultural transmission and dissemination Holloway locates as being at the heart of black cultural sensibility. For despite its role in African-American subject formation, in Holloway's conception the passing on that contributes to one's cultural sensibility is seldom a significant event. It is interwoven with daily life. It is an iconography, a perspective, an expectation. And even though this expectation might bring pleasure, pleasure in identification, pleasure in knowing, there are also ways in which one's identification with another's life—as set forth in the condition for feeling responsible for receiving the news of another's death—can also foreclose one's own possibility for a future.

In a *New York Times Magazine* article titled "Ghetto Miasma: Enough to Make You Sick?" Helen Epstein, a writer of literary non-fiction, asks us to consider the relationship between illness and high death rates in black communities.[6] Even though African Americans, violence, and poverty have become inextricably linked in our popular consciousness, Epstein begins by reminding her reader that illness kills far more African Americans than violence, and in greater proportions than other groups, even when controlling for income and access to health care. And it is particularly difficult,

Epstein argues, to talk about treating illness in blacks because there are so many sources from which illness could arrive. Is it environmental? Economic? Psychological? Is it biological? Psychic? The answer, as Epstein points out, might be "any of the above," or, even more disconcertingly, *all of the above*, particularly as they may all be distilled as a common effect—"stress." Epstein summarizes the ghostliness of this suffering in the term "ghetto miasma," which carries her sense of things that we know are real but cannot see, and of common effects that cannot be returned to singular locations, nor are even diagnosable, *per se*. "Something," Epstein insists, "is killing America's urban poor, but this is no ordinary epidemic." Epstein's willingness to begin with a mere "something" makes it possible to imagine everything, in the process eliciting and then identifying a long series of blows to African-American well-being: the impact of culture on health, the impact of inadequate access to medical care, the impact of racism on doctor-patient relationships, and so on.

When Epstein recounts the tales of young people like Jo-Scama Wontong, who "has lost so many people she loved to disease and accident recently that whenever she thinks about it, she is stricken with panic," I hear Karla Holloway's assertions regarding black cultural sensibility, her assertion that, for African Americans, "the formative years, the waning years, and each day between were haunted by one spiritual's refrain: 'soon one morning, death will come a-calling.'" I hear this in Jo-Scama's revelation that, randomly and unexpectedly, she finds that "My heart beats so fast, and I can't breathe, and there's just death going through my mind the whole time." Her haunting is real, having come to her by virtue of her experiences of living through the deaths of others. Such encroachment is particularly terrifying in Epstein's account because she also offers glimpses into how such haunting is effected systemically, how it moves across different parts of people's lives. When Epstein sets data about impoverished American minorities who have been here for generations against that of poor recent immigrants from the same backgrounds, she finds that the immigrants are generally healthier. "It makes you wonder," she offers, "whether there is something deadly in the American experience of urban poverty itself." This is haunting in its most negative effect, emerging without any sense of how to stop its encroachment, its possession of living.

THE SHADOW OF THE OBJECT

How do people protect themselves against such encroachment? It is a difficult balance, for living on either end of the continuum brings its own more complete despair. On one end there is living with an excess of remembering and knowing, living, to use Bob Kaufman's language, as "Seekers of manifest disembowelment on shafts of yesterday's pains." But on the other end? Living with a painful absence, with a phantom limb.[7] Yet even if one might not be able to control one's environment, cannot alone end racial violence, or steel against the news of other people's deaths, there are indeed ways we seize tiny bits of control, make small spaces of balanced relation, find some distance so that we might live with, Karla Holloway puts it, "grace, hope, and resilience."[8]

At the end of *Beloved* Toni Morrison offers an example of how many manage to live in delicate balance between knowing and knowing enough, between remembering and letting go. Those final pages of her novel are wide and shimmering, as if arriving from a distance, and they offer the following as a narrative for how the novel's ghost disappears from consciousness, regardless of whether she is gone from or has ever been in the material world:

> So they forgot her. Like an unpleasant dream during a troubling sleep. Occasionally, however, the rustle of a skirt hushes when they awake, and the knuckles brushing a cheek in sleep seem to belong to the sleeper. Sometimes the photograph of a close friend or relative—looked at too long—shifts, and something more familiar than the dear face itself moves there. They can touch it if they like, but don't, because they know things will never be the same if they do.[9]

Anachronistic to the time during which most of the action of *Beloved* takes place, Morrison's use of the photograph functions at the end of her novel as a figure through which her characters' experiences of Beloved the ghost and our experience of *Beloved* the novel might be collapsed, for Morrison is commenting on the very acts of viewing, reading, and interpretation that characterize Sethe and others' responses to the ghost and also that we as readers are still engaging at novel's end. Here, Morrison focuses our attention on the gap between what is in a photograph and what we bring to it. What rests in that gap is the possibility that one's relationship to a photo, one's claim on a photo, is in fact a misunderstood relation. Too much looking, looking too long, risks clarifying the true nature of the relation. Melancholic, a photograph is not the loved object. It is the shadow of the object, the relation, "something more familiar than the dear face." You.

Morrison's choice of the photograph as the final figuration in *Beloved* has roots in her interest and collaboration in the work of famous African-American photographer James Van Der Zee. In his work as a photographer of Harlem, James Van Der Zee has provided an important archive of black life in early-to mid-twentieth-century America. His bread and butter, however, lay in his photos of everyday people, of the rich and poor who wanted records of their most important moments: weddings, deaths, and stepping out. His work has been collected in several volumes, perhaps most notably in *The Harlem Book of the Dead*, for which Morrison wrote the foreword. In that book, editor Camille Billops compiles many of Van Der Zee's funeral photographs, many of which also feature one of Van Der Zee's most well-known techniques, which involved burning other images into the photographs, so that they are also collages. Well after the publication of *The Harlem Book of the Dead*, Van Der Zee's photos continued to haunt Morrison's work in general, most notably in *Jazz*, which Morrison says was inspired by one of Van Der Zee's photos of the dead.[10]

Needless to say, any encounter with Van Der Zee's book will likely be a haunting one, for not only are its photos striking on their own account, but knowing that each photo's subject is dead unhinges the photos from easy categorization. Photographing the dead disrupts the assumed temporality of representation, as the anteriority of the subject to its representation suddenly seems less important, less likely, and by virtue of this new perspective also potentially reveals that which is more than a bit creepy in any photograph. In particular, Van Der Zee's photos in *The Harlem Book of the Dead* are especially striking for how they do not quite represent death or dying. As Morrison puts it in her foreword, "The narrative quality, the intimacy, the humanity of his photographs are stunning, and the proof, if any is needed, is in this collection of pictures devoted exclusively to the dead about which one can only say, 'How living are his portraits of the dead.'"[11] As representations of the dead, Van Der Zee's photographs reveal how life is haunted by death in general, a fact perhaps best symbolized in the idea of the photograph, a displacement that nonetheless allows us to turn away, to instead experience pleasure in memory.

"FUTURE EXPECTATIONS"

If Van Der Zee's photographs of the dead disrupt the temporality of representation in their uncanny vivification of the dead, there is also a way in which his technique also opens disruption in the opposite direction. Such is the case with "Future Expectations (Harlem Wedding)," a wedding picture into which Van Der Zee has burned an image of a young girl holding a doll (figure 2). Unarrived, she appears as a future blessing to the newly wed. This sense of blessing is deepened by the sincerity of her visage in relation to the *trompe l'œil* backdrop with which the original photograph was taken. In *trompe l'œil*, linear perspective creates an illusion of depth by tricking the eye into seeing a future in what is not in fact visible, for instance the convergence of a pair of lines moving away from the viewer and into the distance. If those lines were to in fact meet as we imagine they do, at their vanishing point, that place would also be a place of absolute collapse.

We might think here of Jean Toomer's "Carma." As the narrator watches Carma, heading on down a dusty road in Georgia, she "disappears in a cloudy rumble at some indefinite point along the road."[12] He is looking too hard, and under the heavy weight of his gaze the image of her collapses as she passes on to a place that had in fact never been marked in visible space. In Van Der Zee's studio, the backdrop gives dimension to his clients' poses, producing scenes of comfort and luxury that are likely foreign to their material circumstances. *But that doesn't matter*, the little girl seems to say by her presence. She, like the twin hearts etched in the fireplace and visually echoed in the bow on her head, is here to remind us that this love has a future, despite its present exigencies.

Figure 2 James Van Der Zee, "Future Expectations (Harlem Wedding)", Gelatin silver print, printed 1974 [1926]. High Museum of Art, Atlanta; Purchase, 74.143 L.

But here too is a possibility for collapse. At second glance, the couple seems very young; the bride even younger. Yet despite their youth or the conceptual luxury of their surroundings, the bride's feet are swollen. The scale is off; the shoes too tight, or too unfamiliar for work-a-day feet, much as the dress is equally too big. Not hers. Her eyes, beautiful, are a touch too serious, looking too far out of the frame. What does she know that he does not? That we will never know? All these tiny excesses: the bride has too much veil, the imaginary doll is big as the imaginary child; there is too much space where the edges of the scene should meet, the fire too lovely with its tendrils. But the bride's gaze is also calm, and the groom's mouth is so tender, ready to smile. Despite the artifice through which the image has been constructed, in my belief that this couple is real I also come to believe that they will indeed find happiness. Perhaps the hesitation has been all mine, and, with another look, I am unsure how much I should care about veracity, much less the meaning of these tiny excesses. Moving away, just a touch, I again feel a real affection.

I cannot help but think here of Julie Dash's film, *Daughters of the Dust*, which is narrated by an unborn child.[13] Her ghostly presence simultaneously signifies the past and the present: the pain of her mother's rape at the hands of a white man; the hope for the future embodied in her young parents' marriage; the danger of transition from the spirit world to the world of the living; and as well the dangerous migration from island life to mainland life her Gullah family is about to make. In the care and exuberance of her narration we might come to understand how one might meet a ghost with grace and graciousness, and how simultaneously similar and dissimilar the past must always remain, remainder, from the future. Yet unborn but not untried, she sings the film's thematic chorus: "I remember and I recall." Understanding recovery, understanding how lives might again become livable after terrible events, is necessary to the interpretation of any art growing out of such events. *I remember and I recall*, and this too must be claimed.

It don't stop til we complete this,
keep this, fly
There's so much to life when you just stay Black and die

Blacker than the nighttime sky of Bed-Stuy in July
Blacker than the seed in the blackberry pie. . .

Notes

NOTES TO THE INTRODUCTION

1. Toni Morrison, *Jazz* (New York: Plume, 1993), 228.
2. Jacques Derrida, *Specters of Marx: The State of the Debt, the Work of Mourning and the New International*, trans. Peggy Kamuf (London: Routledge, 1994), 16.
3. Dominick La Capra, *Writing History, Writing Trauma* (Baltimore, MD: John Hopkins Press, 2001), 27.
4. Saidiya V. Hartman, *Scenes of Subjection: Terror, Slavery, and Self-Making in Nineteenth-Century America* (New York: Oxford University Press, 1997). Hartman's argument revolves around figures like Paul Rankin, a well-known nineteenth-century abolitionist whom she takes to task for his displays of empathy for the enslaved, during which he expresses his abolitionist sentiments via protracted narratives focused on what it would be like if he and his family were slaves. Hartman has some sympathy for Rankin's strategy, noting that "By believing himself to be and by phantasmically becoming the enslaved, he created the scenario for shared feelings" (Hartman, 18). But she finds in Rankin's "empathic identification" a troubling, if not dangerous, possession:

   > In the fantasy of being beaten, Rankin must substitute himself and his wife and children for the black captive in order that this pain be perceived and experienced. So, in fact, Rankin becomes a proxy and the other's pain is acknowledged to the degree that it can be imagined, yet by virtue of this substitution the object of identification threatens to disappear. (Hartman, 19)

   According to Hartman, Rankin's strategy guarantees that the proper subjects of his narratives, slaves, never in fact appear, having instead been transmuted into figures with whom his audience can easily identify—themselves, which thus repeats the objectification that characterizes the plight of the very people he seeks to save, as the victim, now a mere object, disappears. In Hartman's view, "the endeavor to bring pain close," also "increases the difficulty of beholding black suffering" itself (Hartman, 20).
5. Dori Laub, *Testimony: Crises of Witnessing in Literature, Psychoanalysis and History* (New York: Routledge, 1991), 58.
6. James Baldwin, "Every Good-Bye Ain't Gone," in *Collected Essays*, ed. Toni Morrison (New York: Library of America, 1998), 775.
7. Cf. Stuart Hall, "Minimal Selves," *Black British Cultural Studies: A Reader*, eds. Houston A. Baker, Jr., Manthia Diawara, and Ruth H. Lindeborg (Chicago: University of Chicago Press, 1996). Also see Jacques Lacan, "The Mirror Stage as Formative of the Function of the *I*" and "Aggressivity in Psychoanalysis," in *Écrits: A Selection* (New York: W.W. Norton, 1997).
8. Toni Morrison, *Beloved: A Novel* (New York: Penguin, 1998), 36.
9. James Baldwin, *The Fire Next Time* in *Collected Essays*, 342.
10. "Hanging of black teen conjures up dark memories in Mississippi," Associate Press News Service, July 18, 2000, http://archives.cnn.com/2000/US/07/18/mississippi.hanging.ap/ Also see Kevin Sack, "U.S. Assures Jesse Jackson It Is Pursuing Death of a Black Mississippi Youth," *New York Times*, July 13, 2000.

11. Christopher Metress, ed., "Afterword," *The Lynching of Emmett Till: A Documentary Narrative* (University of Virginia Press, 2002), 346.
12. Pierre Nora, "Between Memory and History: *Les Lieux De Mémoire*," trans. Lawrence D. Kritzman, *Realms of Memory: Rethinking the French Past* (New York: Columbia University Press, 1996). In his introduction to the English language edition of *Les Frances*, distributed as *Realms of Memory*, Nora insists that by looking "beyond the historical reality" of text, place, and tradition, one could "discover the symbolic reality and recover the memory that it sustained." This notion, that our historical objects are for the most part constructed rather than collected, marked a departure from the archival reconstruction that characterizes modern historical writing's most recognizable valance, and also laid the groundwork for new ways of talking about the life of the past in public discourse, as *Les Frances* offers up "memory" as a way of reconciling the problems of history in the age of identity politics. To accomplish this, Nora put into scholarly practice the more theoretical work he had done with Jacques LeGoff and others towards articulating the differences between memory and history, in the end coming down on the side of memory.
13. It is important to note that determining the construction and deployment of sites of memory is a cross-disciplinary concern, and has come to a great variety of expression in African-American literature and culture. For an excellent interdisciplinary survey, see the essays collected in Robert O'Meally and Genevieve Fabre, eds., *History and Memory in African-American Culture* (New York: Oxford University Press, 1994), and also Elizabeth Rauh Bethel, *The Roots of African-American Identity: Memory and History in Antebellum Free Communities* (New York: Palgrave Macmillan, 1999).
14. Allan H. Spear, *Black Chicago: The Making of A Negro Ghetto* (Chicago: University of Chicago Press, 1967), vii.
15. Ellen O'Brien and Lyle Benedict, "1919: Race Riots," in *Deaths, Disturbances, Disasters and Disorders in Chicago: A Selective Bibliography of Materials from the Municipal Reference Collection of the Chicago Public Library*. 2001 [1996]. Available: http://www.chipublib.org/004chicago/disasters/riots_race.html
16. William M. Tuttle, *Race Riot: Chicago in the Red Summer of 1919* (Urbana: University of Illinois Press, 1996), 4–7.
17. Peter M. Hoffman, Cook County (Ill.) Coroner, *The Race Riots: Biennial Report 1918–1919*. Available: http://www.chipublib.org/004chicago/disasters/text/coroner/17.html

NOTES TO CHAPTER 1

1. Édouard Glissant, "The Known, The Uncertain," trans. J. Michael Dash, in *Caribbean Discourse: Selected Essays* (Charlottesville: University Press of Virginia, 1989).
2. Melvin Dixon, "The Black Writer's Use of Memory," in *History and Memory in African-American Culture*, eds. Robert O'Meally and Geneviève Fabre (New York: Oxford University Press, 1994), 20.
3. Dixon, "Memory," 21.
4. Karla F. C. Holloway, *Passed On: African American Mourning Stories: A Memorial* (Durham: Duke University Press, 2002), 6.
5. Olaudah Equiano, "The Interesting Narrative of the Life of Olaudah Equiano," in *Black Atlantic Writers of the Eighteenth Century*, eds. Adam Potkay and Sandra Burr (New York: St. Martin's Press, 1995), 185.

6. Quobna Ottoba Cugoano, "Thoughts and Sentiments on the Evil and Wicked Traffic of the Commerce of the Human Species," in *Black Atlantic Writers*, 134.
7. Equiano, 186.
8. Equiano, 186.
9. See Langston Hughes, *The Big Sea*, 2 vols. (New York: Thunder's Mouth Press, 1986), 1:50.
10. Hughes, *Big Sea*, 54, 55. I find it interesting that Hughes's nostalgia is not unlike Pierre Nora's, whom I discuss at more length in the introduction and chapter 2 of this book. Nora makes repeated references to *milieux de mémoire* as environments in which one would experience living in "the warmth of tradition" and "the silence of custom" (Nora, 7). Both men at times hearken to a belief in the embedded authenticity of a pre-modern, premigration world. For Nora, this world in which living is real and meaningful is located squarely amongst the rural class; for Hughes, it is with Southerners, particularly those who would become the newly migrated working-class people whom he both envied and admired.
11. Hughes, *Big Sea*, 118.
12. The difference, of course, is that whereas the Middle Passage signifies a passage between continents, being "sold down the river" signifies a second (and third and fourth . . .) passage that happens entirely on American soil. Regardless, as Farah Griffin and others have explained, the journey remains constitutive of post-Passage subjectivity. Farah Jasmine Griffin, "*Who Set You Flowin'?": The African-American Migration Narrative* (New York: Oxford University Press, 1995).
13. Langston Hughes, "The Negro Speaks of Rivers," in *The Collected Poems of Langston Hughes*, ed. Arnold Rampersad (New York: Knopf, 1994), lines 1–3. All subsequent Hughes poems are from this edition and will be cited parenthetically by line number.
14. Julia Kristeva, *Revolution in Poetic Language*, trans. Margaret Walker (New York: Columbia University Press, 1984), 57.
15. Kristeva, 48.
16. Kristeva, 58.
17. Hughes, *Big Sea*, 118.
18. I am not suggesting here that Pey speaks as an authentic African who actually holds the power to determine Hughes's racial membership. Rather, what I am interested in is the validation Hughes wants from Pey, and the way that Pey—even if it could be read as a misrecognition on his part—refuses to give it.
19. Hortense J. Spillers, "Mama's Baby, Papa's Maybe: An American Grammar Book," in *Diacritics* 17.2 (1987): 72.
20. Arnold Rampersad, *The Life of Langston Hughes*, 2 vols. (New York: Oxford University Press, 1986), 1:78. For Hughes, the impossibility of identification with a racially homogeneous origin would become a pervasive concern throughout his career; see Rampersad, 1:82.
21. Dixon, "Memory," 24.
22. Countee Cullen, "Heritage," in *My Soul's High Song: The Collected Writings of Countee Cullen*, ed. and intro. Gerald Early (New York: Doubleday, 1991), lines 31–37. Hereafter cited parenthetically by line number.
23. Dixon, "Memory," 24.
24. Early, introduction to *My Soul's High Song*, 59–60.
25. Toni Morrison, "The Site of Memory," in *Inventing the Truth: The Art and Craft of Memoir*, ed. William Zinsser (Boston: Houghton Mifflin, 1987), 119.
26. I say more on this in chapter 2 of this book.

27. Paul de Man, “The Rhetoric of Temporality,” in *Blindness and Insight: Essays in the Rhetoric of Contemporary Criticism* (Minneapolis: University of Minnesota Press, 1983), 207.
28. Morrison, 119.
29. Morrison, 120.
30. Helene Johnson, “Poem,” in *This Waiting for Love: Helene Johnson, Poet of the Harlem Renaissance,* ed. Verner D. Mitchell (Amherst, MA: University of Massachusetts Press, 2006), lines 1–13. Hereafter cited parenthetically by line number. I also continue my discussion of Johnson’s “Poem” in the following chapter.

NOTES TO CHAPTER 2

1. James Baldwin, “The Discovery of What It Means To Be An American,” in *Collected Essays*, ed. Toni Morrison (New York: Library of America, 1998), 138.
2. Helene Johnson, “Poem,” in *This Waiting for Love: Helene Johnson, Poet of the Harlem Renaissance*, ed. Verner D. Mitchell (Amherst, MA: University of Massachusetts Press, 2006). Hereafter cited parenthetically by line number.
3. Pierre Nora, “Between Memory and History: *Les Lieux De Mémoire,*” trans. Marc Roudebush, *Representations,* no. 26 (1989), 7. From this now famous assertion radiates the tenor and content of Nora’s lament. It is perhaps the signal-call of his own incipient nostalgia, for there is a sense that *Les Frances,* simultaneously representative and constitutive, would be able to articulate out of the vicissitudes of modern existence sustaining relationships between nation, history and identity. The world that Nora claims as lost was an essentially pre-modern, pre-migration world where tradition and emplacement engendered and enriched a citizen’s lived experience of memory, an intact world in which living did the work of collective memory, which in turn did the proper work of history—that is, made citizens, the people who remember *why.*
4. Nora, 7. “Now,” however, there is only history, a never-ending stretch of archival documentation that is at its heart antagonistic to memory. In Nora’s construction, “history” is best understood as what Nietzsche would dub “monumental history,” which names the special function of state memory, a kind of history that cannot be questioned as it pulls difference and dissent into its combine. History: static, structured, and firmly closed to discourse by virtue of its constantly reified distance from the present. Memory, conversely: fluid, critical, and magical in its ability to transform the past and its onlooker; it is “a perpetually actual phenomenon, a bond tying us to the eternal present” (Nora, 8). According to Nora, then, history can never be more than merely the past’s pastness. Also see Friedrich Wilhelm Nietzsche, *On the Advantage and Disadvantage of History for Life* (Indianapolis: Hackett Publishing Company, 1980).
5. Nora, 8–9. In his introduction to Maurice Halbwachs’ *On Collective Memory,* translator Lewis Coser notes that Halbwachs was “determined to demolish Bergson’s stress on subjective time and individual consciousness. . . .” and that Halbwachs’ theory of memory hinged on the fact that “We are never alone” (Halbwachs, 23). Accordingly, an individual’s memory cannot exist independently of a greater collective memory; and for Halbwachs, this phenomena finds its most salient example in the interplay of individual and collective within the family structure. To be intelligible, each memory must

be located "within the thought of the corresponding group" (Halbwachs, 53). Halbwachs arrives at his thesis through a comparison of individual memory as it appears in dreams versus its appearance in the waking state: "The dream is based only on itself, whereas our recollections depend on those of all our fellow, and on the great frameworks of the memory of society" (Halbwachs, 42). Memories remembered while dreaming are recollected without the "consistency, depth, coherence, or stability" that characterizes the recollection of an awake individual, which points to how consciousness of community shapes remembering (Halbwachs, 44). Maurice Halbwachs, *On Collective Memory*. trans. Lewis A. Coser (Chicago: University of Chicago Press, 1992). Per Bergson, Henri Bergson, *Matter and Memory* (New York: Zone Books, 1988). Also see, Gilles Deleuze, *Bergsonism* (New York: Zone Books, 1990). On this sense that remembering is impacted by community structures, also see Roberta Culbertson, "Embodied Memory, Transcendence, and Telling: Recounting Trauma, Re-Establishing the Self," in *New Literary History* 26.1 (1995): 169–95. I also take up Culbertson and Bergson more extensively in chapter five of this book, "Saying Yes."

6. Nora, 9. I take this notion of "cultural sensibility" from Karla Holloway, whom I discuss more extensively in the conclusion to this book. Karla F. C. Holloway, *Passed On: African American Mourning Stories: A Memorial* (Durham: Duke University Press, 2002).
7. James Baldwin, *Another Country* (New York: Vintage Books, 1993). This can also be read in relation to the trope of the American jazz club as a heterotopic space, a space outside of which a person might be destroyed for the very thing that, for reasons of race or sexuality, he or she was first drawn to the club's alterity in the first place. For more on the heterotopic, see Michel Foucault, "Of Other Spaces," in *Diacritics*, Vol. 16, No. 1 (Spring, 1986), 22–27.
8. Baldwin, *Another Country*, 27. I am reminded here of Jean Toomer's Becky, a Southern white woman who is impregnated twice by an unidentified black man. The responses of both blacks and whites are described as being said by their mouths, rather than by the people *per se*: "Damn buck nigger, said the white folks' mouths"; "Poor Catholic poor-white crazy woman, said the black folks' mouths" (Toomer, "Becky," 7). By moving agency to the mechanism of dissemination, the mouths, rather than having that speaking emerge from people, Toomer highlights a sense of social values to which all must adhere, even as no one is openly willing to take responsibility for the enactment of those values. This separation between word and origin is also a figure for the gap between how Becky is treated publicly and how she is treated privately. She is a pariah, kept fed and sheltered by individuals who must remain anonymous in their simultaneous acts of kindness and cruelty, kept out sight as "White folks and black folks built her cabin, fed her and her growing baby . . ." (Toomer, "Becky," 7). Literally and figuratively pushed to the town's edge—Toomer describes her cabin as set "between the road and the railroad track"—Becky is a ghost who haunts the boundaries between social value and private desire. By *enforcing* her ghostliness, the town allows her meaning to circulate, even as they also refuse address. Jean Toomer, "Becky," in *Cane*, Darwin T. Turner, ed. (New York: W.W. Norton, 1988).
9. Baldwin, *Another Country*, 5.
10. Baldwin, *Another Country*, 121.
11. Baldwin, *Another Country*, 8–9, passim.
12. Baldwin, *Another Country*, 296.
13. Toni Morrison, *Song of Solomon* (New York: Alfred A. Knopf, 1994), 331.
14. Baldwin, *Another Country*, 8–9.

15. Baldwin, *Another Country*, 128.
16. Baldwin, *Another Country*, 8–9, passim.
17. Such interweaving is found throughout the text, though my analysis will continue this chapter's focus on "Book One: Easy Rider" of *Another Country*, which mainly follows the days leading up to Rufus' death and its immediate aftermath.
18. Baldwin, *Another Country*, 49–51, passim.
19. Baldwin, *Another Country*, 59.
20. Baldwin, *Another Country*, 415.
21. Baldwin, *Another Country*, 19.
22. Written by black songwriter Andy Razaf, "(What Did I Do to Be So) Black and Blue?" was originally composed for an all-black revue, financed by a gangster wanting "something with a little colored girl singing how tough it is being colored," (O'Meally, quoting Barry Singer). O'Meally reads the song as potentially the first racial protest song in the United States, for it is "a site of contestation over the meaning of black expression and history. Schultz called for minstrel-show style Negro pathos and received, from Razaf, a protest song gently ribboned in humor; Armstrong edited out the humor to intensify the protest song's racial edge and tragic thrust" (O'Meally, 129). Robert O'Meally, "Checking Our Balances: Ellison on Armstrong's Humor," *boundary 2* (2003), 30:2.
23. Louis Armstrong and His Orchestra, "(What Did I Do to Be So) Black and Blue?" *The Hot Fives & Sevens* [Disc 4]. (JSP Records, 1999).
24. Baldwin, *Another Country*, 12–13.
25. Baldwin, *Another Country*, 6–7.
26. Baldwin, *Another Country*, 50–53, passim.
27. Baldwin, *Another Country*, 51. Thanks to one of my students, Joseph Silver, who pointed me to the resonance between Razaf's original version of "Black and Blue," and Bessie Smith's "Empty Bed Blues." J. Silver, "Ghost Notes of a Native Son" (undergraduate thesis, Amherst College, 2008), 15.
28. Baldwin, *Another Country*, 17.
29. Baldwin, *Another Country*, 416.
30. Baldwin, *Another Country*, 87.
31. Albert Murray, *Stomping the Blues* (New York: Da Capo, 1989 [1987]), 45.
32. Murray, 51, 17.
33. Adam Gussow, *Seems Like Murder Here: Southern Violence and the Blues Tradition* (Chicago: University of Chicago Press, 2002), 137.
34. Paul de Man, *Blindness and Insight: Essays in the Rhetoric of Contemporary Criticism* (Minneapolis: University of Minnesota Press, 1993), 207. Also see the discussion of Countee Cullen in chapter 1 of this book.
35. Angela Davis, *Blues Legacies and Black Feminism: Gertrude "Ma" Rainey, Bessie Smith, and Billie Holiday* (New York: Vintage, 1999), 111.
36. Bessie Smith, "Backwater Blues [1927]," *The Essential Bessie Smith.* (SMG, 1997).
37. Baldwin, *Another Country*, 70.
38. Davis, 109.
39. Toni Morrison, "The Site of Memory" in *Inventing the Truth: The Art and Craft of* Memoir, ed. William Zinsser (Boston: Houghton Mifflin, 1987). I take this up more extensively in chapter 1 of this book.
40. Toni Morrison, *Beloved: A Novel.* (New York: Penguin, 1998), 36. I take up this sense of rememory in the introduction to this book.
41. There is a wide variety of texts available on this matter. Per this analysis, John M. Barry, *Rising Tide: The Great Mississippi Flood of 1927 and How It Changed America* (Simon & Schuster: New York, 1998) is particularly

useful. For a consideration of the 1927 flood in relation to Smith's "Backwater Blues," also see David Evans, "Bessie Smith's 'Back-Water Blues': The Story Behind the Song," *Popular Music* (2006), 26: 97–116.

42. Baldwin, *Another Country*, 87.
43. Melvin Dixon, *Ride Out the Wilderness: Geography and Identity in Afro-American Literature* (Urbana: University of Illinois Press, 1987), 132.
44. Baldwin, *Another Country*, 78.
45. Baldwin, *Another Country*, 83–87, passim.
46. Baldwin, *Another Country*, 87.
47. Baldwin, *Another Country*, 119.

NOTES TO CHAPTER 3

1. Jean Toomer, "Cotton Song," in *Cane*, ed. Darwin T. Turner (New York: W.W. Norton, 1988).
2. Bessie Smith, "Jailhouse Blues [1923]," in *The Blues: Smithsonian Collection Of Classic Blues Singers* (Smithsonian Collection, 1993).
3. James Baldwin. *Another Country* (New York: Vintage Books, 1993), 82.
4. In her introduction to *Split-Gut Song*, Karen Jackson Ford has a nice survey of some of the dominant critical takes on the question of what is at stake in how one describes and understands generic form in *Cane*. Karen Jackson Ford, *Split-Gut Song*: *Jean Toomer and the Poetics of Modernity*. (Tuscaloosa, AL: University of Alabama Press, 2005).
5. Nathaniel Mackey. *Discrepant Engagement: Dissonance, Cross-Culturality, and Experimental Writing*. (New York: Cambridge University Press, 2000), 239.
6. Toomer, "Karintha," 4.
7. This is also a function of the kaleidoscopic geometry of the book's form more generally, which heavily depends on montage, especially in its first section. Montage, with its ruptures, juxtapositions, and found objects, creates in *Cane* a temporal sensibility grounded specifically in the moment of reading, an orientation towards the present that asks readers to experience Toomer's text with memory's force, in what Joel Peckham has referred to as "a dialectic in which the artist invites the viewer to explore the ruptures caused by placing divergent or discordant elements together" (Peckham, 288). Toomer's use of montage as the dominant formal structure of the novel's first third requires that the reader keep his or her reading in the present, in the sense that dialectical reading names a process in which the reader comes to meaning through an active negotiation of blank spaces; one can only fill in the blanks with what one has. In the event of reading, the reader is projected into the moment of textualization. By memorializing, collecting all these pieces, but not monumentalizing the South, by *not* positing it as a single, solid thing that one could refer to and declare, "this was it," Toomer gives us something mobile, rich, and glossable, a text that can be approached in numerous ways and accessed at any point—a book of memory. Joel Peckham, "Jean Toomer's *Cane*: Self as Montage and the Drive Toward Integration," in *American Literature* 72.2 (2000): 275–90.
8. Toomer, "Carma," 12.
9. I elaborate this sense of *milieu de mémoire* in chapter 2 of this book.
10. Toomer, "Carma," 12.
11. This posteriority can also be tied into Angela Davis' notion of the political possibilities engendered by "aesthetic distance," the distance between an event and its representation, as discussed in chapter 2 of this book. In Toni

Morrison's *Beloved*, one can also detect a similar sense of posteriority—of an expression or experience specifically located in an event that comes *after* an equally specific event—in Sethe's invocation of the "you" in her description of rememory. In that example, a person's encounter with a haunted site supposedly trumps spatial and temporal distance, which nonetheless makes a political possibility similar to what Davis imagines as potential in aesthetic distance. Angela Davis. *Blues Legacies and Black Feminism: Gertrude "Ma" Rainey, Bessie Smith, and Billie Holiday* (New York: Vintage, 1999).

12. This could also be understood as a literary articulation of Henri Bergson's notion of "pure duration." Henri Bergson, *Matter and Memory* (New York: Zone Books, 1998). Further, this recourse to gerund experience reveals an effect not unlike what Julia Kristeva refers to as the function of poetic language, language that, in its fragmentation, enacts verisimilitude by referring only to itself, in "the language of materiality as opposed to transparency," in the truth claim of the moment's moment (Kristeva, 28). I take this up more extensively in chapter 1 of this book. Julia Kristeva, *Revolution in Poetic Language*, trans. Margaret Waller (New York: Columbia University Press, 1984).
13. Toomer, "Carma," 12.
14. David M. Oshinsky, *Worse Than Slavery: Parchman Farm and the Ordeal of Jim Crow Justice* (New York: Free Press, 1996). I want to note that I am not putting "Rosie" forth as a sociological object, but I do think that this rendition of the song captures in its sound a particular kind of tension between longing and anxiety germane to "Carma." Unlike much of *Cane*'s music, genre-similar recordings like "Rosie" are available to us today. And like the Billie Holiday and Bessie Smith songs that provide the basic texture for feeling in *Another Country*, "Rosie" offers us a sample of the kinds of sounds that would have informed *Cane*'s conception and writing.
15. C.B. and Axe Gang, "Rosie," *The Alan Lomax Collection: Prison Songs, Vol. 1—Murderous Home, 1947–1948* (Rounder Records, 1997).
16. Oshinsky, 146. It is important to keep in mind Parchman Farm's structural reliance on its plantation system, a direct carryover from slavery. David Oshinsky gives a useful account of this connection, particularly in chapter five. Also see William Banks Taylor, *Down on Parchman Farm: The Great Prison in the Mississippi Delta* (Columbus, OH: Ohio State University Press, 1999), especially chapter three.
17. Specifically how the law's refusal to protect slave domesticity was concomitant with its implicit support of the rape of black slaves. For a cultural studies/ legal perspective, see for instance Kimberlé Crenshaw, "Mapping the Margins: Intersectionality, Identity Politics, and Violence Against Women of Color," 43 *Stanford Law Review*: 1241 (1993). Also see, Deborah Gray White, *Ar'n't I a Woman?: Female Slaves in the Plantation South* (New York: W. W. Norton, 1999).
18. Toomer, "Carma," 12.
19. Baldwin, *Another Country*, 7.
20. Pierre Nora, "Between Memory and History: *Les Lieux De Mémoire*," trans. Marc Roudebush, in *Representations*, 26 (1989), 12.

NOTES TO CHAPTER 4

1. W.E.B. Dubois, *The Souls of Black Folk* (New York: Knopf, 1993).
2. Marcel Proust, *Swann's Way* (New York: Vintage Books, 1989).
3. Toni Morrison, *Beloved: A Novel* (New York: Penguin, 1998), 36.
4. I take this up more explicitly in the introduction to this book.

5. Proust, 60.
6. Proust, 61.
7. Proust, 64.
8. Bob Kaufman, "I Have Folded My Sorrows," in *Solitudes Crowded with Loneliness* (New York: New Directions Publishing Corporation, 1965), lines 1–3. Hereafter cited parenthetically by line number.
9. William Wordsworth, *The Prose Works of William Wordsworth, Vol. 2*, eds. Owen and Jane Worthington Smyser (Oxford: Clarendon, 1974).
10. Countee Cullen, "Heritage," in *My Soul's High Song: The Collected Writings of Countee Cullen*, ed. Gerald Early (New York: Doubleday, 1991), lines 27–30. I have a more extensive discussion of the Cullen poem in chapter 2 of this book.
11. Nathaniel Mackey, *Discrepant Engagement: Dissonance, Cross-Culturality, and Experimental Writing* (New York: Cambridge University Press, 1993), 240.
12. Pierre Nora, "Between Memory and History: *Les Lieux De Mémoire,*" trans. Marc Roudebush, *Representations,* Spring, no 26 (1989): 7. I discuss Nora's notion of *le milieu* in chapter 2 of this book.
13. Jean Toomer, "Song of the Son," in *Cane*, ed. Darwin T. Turner (New York: W.W. Norton, 1988), 14.
14. Barbara Johnson, "Apostrophe, Animation, and Abortion," in *Diacritics*, 16.1 (Spring, 1986), 28–47.
15. Charles Scruggs, "Jean Toomer and Kenneth Burke and the Persistence of the Past" in *American Literary History* 13.1 (2001), 49.
16. In pursuit of the Christian thematic, one might also note that the poem's five stanzas could be read as arriving at the fifth station of the cross, which commonly represents the scene of Simon of Cyrene, a passerby made to carry Jesus' cross as he is carried to his crucifixion (Mark 15:21). Simon of Cyrene has also been claimed by some as the first African saint, which also tinges the poem's Christian imagery with a memory of African presence.
17. Jean Toomer, "Carma" in *Cane,* ed. Darwin T. Turner (New York: W.W. Norton, 1988), 12.
18. As Susan Edmunds has pointed out, despite critical attempts to associate Toomer's *Cane* with stereotypes of a politically detached literary modernism, the text should be understood explicitly in the context of a black middle class deeply invested in activism motivated by the fight against lynching. Edmunds reads Toomer, and particularly "Song of the Son," as inseparable from the world of anti-lynching politics and "the wider African American discourses and print communities without which, by their own account, *Cane* itself would not exist." Susan Edmunds, "The Race Question and the 'Question of the Home': Revisiting the Lynching Plot in Jean Toomer's *Cane*," in *American Literature*, 75.1 (March 2003), 142.

NOTES TO CHAPTER 5

1. Linda Hogan, *The Woman Who Watches Over the World: A Native Memoir* (New York: W.W. Norton, 2001), 196.
2. Lisa Long, "A Relative Pain: The Rape of History in Octavia Butler's *Kindred* and Phyllis Alesia Perry's *Stigmata*," *College English* 64.4 (2002): 464.
3. Toni Morrison, *Beloved: A Novel* (New York: Penguin, 1998), 36.
4. When I teach Harriet Jacobs' *Incidents in the Life of a Slave Girl*, I do an exercise in which I ask students if what Mr. Flint (Jacobs' owner who spends years trying to make her his concubine) feels for Jacob's could be called love.

They are always at first horrified by my question, but it accomplishes the goal; to consider the question, the narrative's players have to be brought into an uncanny relation: reading the scripts of power and rape and coercion and even terror often seems straightforward for students, because they are already looking for those relations. But upon this kind of reading, Harriet Jacobs, whom they always immediately script only as victim, unexpectedly emerges more fully as an agent, an emergence only possible through a consideration of Mr. Flint's human feeling toward her, as horrifying and ugly as it may be.

5. Octavia Butler, *Kindred* (Boston: Beacon Press, 1988), 13–14.
6. Keith Gilyard, "Genopsycholinguisticide and the Language Theme in African-American Fiction," in *College English* 52.7 (1990): 778.
7. Charles H. Rowell, "An Interview with Octavia B. Butler," in *Callaloo* 20.1 (1997): 51, passim.
8. Interestingly, the project of making history apparent is also *Kindred*'s greatest weakness, as the text often finds itself trapped between fiction and history. There are moments when pedagogy, history's recuperative goal, proves itself *Kindred*'s literary undoing, as at times the novel's tone is a little too pedantic, invoking slavery's written history in a way that seems less intertextual than recitational. The instance when she recites Harriet Tubman's multiple successful escapes is an example of this.
9. Robert Crossley, introduction to *Kindred*, xx-xxii.
10. Butler, 13.
11. Butler, 17.
12. Crossley, xix.
13. Speaking of synonymies, it is hard not to note how much of Dana's working life is based on Butler's. In her interview with Charles Rowell, Butler points out that many of the soul-killing jobs Dana holds in *Kindred* are the same kind of jobs Butler herself worked at to keep a roof over her head. But the coincidence that is most interesting comes from Butler's response to the kind of work her own mother, a domestic, wanted Butler to obtain: "Her big dream for me was that I should get a job as a secretary and be able to sit down when I worked. My big dream was never to be a secretary in my life. I mean, it just seemed such an appallingly servile job, and it turned out to be in a lot of ways. I can remember watching television, which is something, of course, that my mother as a child never had access to, and seeing secretaries on television rushing to do their bosses' bidding and feeling the whole thing to be really kind of humiliating" (Rowell, 51). Dana is also encouraged to go to secretarial school, which she hates and soon drops out of, choosing instead to work as a temp (which is interesting in its own right, as Dana and her colleagues in *Kindred* dub the temp agency they work for "the slave market.") Also, as Kevin becomes more successful, he asks her more often to take care of secretarial tasks for him, an indicator, perhaps, of the nonetheless skewed balance of power in their otherwise equal relationship, as she ends up performing for him tasks she had before rejected.
14. Butler, 22.
15. Butler, 17.
16. Butler, 36.
17. Butler, 177.
18. Roberta Culbertson, "Embodied Memory, Transcendence, and Telling: Recounting Trauma, Re-Establishing the Self," in *New Literary History* 26.1 (1995), 178.
19. Culbertson, 177.
20. Henri Bergson, *Matter and Memory* (New York: Zone Books, 1988), 135.

21. Bergson, 140.
22. Culbertson, 178. Culbertson emphasizes the dangers inherent to this process, explaining that "The demands of narrative for their part operate in fact as cultural silencers to this sort of memory, descending immediately upon an experience to shape notions of legitimate memory, and silencing the sort of proto-memory described. We lose sight of the body's own recall of its response to threat and pain, and of the ways in which it 'speaks' this pain, because this wordless language is unintelligible to one whose body is not similarly affected, and because without words the experience has a certain shadowy quality, a paradoxical unreality" (Culbertson, 178).
23. Nathaniel Mackey, *Discrepant Engagement: Dissonance, Cross-Culturality, and Experimental Writing* (New York: Cambridge University Press, 1993), 235.
24. I say more about the term "real environment of memory" in chapter 2 of this book.
25. Culbertson, 179.
26. Butler, 51.

NOTES TO CHAPTER 6

1. Avery F. Gordon, *Ghostly Matters: Haunting and the Sociological Imagination* (Minneapolis: University of Minnesota Press, 1997), 17.
2. James Baldwin, "Many Thousands Gone," in *Collected Essays*, ed. Toni Morrison (New York: Library of America, 1998), 32.
3. Lawrie Balfour, '"A Most Disagreeable Mirror': Race Consciousness as Double Consciousness," in *Political Theory*, Vol. 26, No. 3. (Jun., 1998), 356.
4. In "Many Thousands Gone," the essay from which the epigraph above is taken, Baldwin is following up on concerns against Wright first addressed in "Everybody's Protest Novel," in which he lumps Wright in with Harriet Beecher Stowe, and the politically problematic values of American racial sentimentalism more generally.
5. Richard Wright, introduction to Horace R. Cayton and St. Clair Drake, *Black Metropolis: A Study of Negro Life in a Northern City* (Chicago: University of Chicago, 1993), xx.
6. Wright, introduction to *Black Metropolis*, xvii.
7. Farah Jasmine Griffin, *Who Set You Flowin?": The African-American Migration Narrative* (New York: Oxford University Press, 1995), 73.
8. It is important to historicize this understanding of art and science in Wright's oeuvre because it changes over the course of his career, as Wright became more willing to consider the limits of social science (a transformation that is surely linked to his changed relationship to Communism). For instance in his introduction to *The Color Curtain*, written fifteen years after *Native Son*, Wright would describe his first reaction to the Bandung Conference as follows:

   > This smacked of something new, something beyond Left and Right. Looked at in terms of history, these nations represented *races* and *religions*, vague but potent forces.

   It was the kind of meeting that no anthropologist, no political scientist would have ever dreamed of staging; it was too simple, too elementary, cutting through the outer layers of disparate social and political facts down to the bare brute residue of human existence: races and religions and continents. [. . . .] There was something extra-political, extra-social, almost extra-human about it; it smacked of tidal waves, of natural forces . . .

Here, race and religion have become "vague" and "potent," forces that now admittedly elude the social scientist. *Now*, he seems to be saying, *that the brown people are doing the writing*. Richard Wright, *The Color Curtain: A Report On The Bandung Conference* (Jackson: University Press of Mississippi, 1995 [1956]).

9. Jean-François Lyotard, *The Differend: Phrases in Dispute* (Minneapolis: University of Minnesota Press, 1988). Lyotard gives the term "differend" to name "a case of conflict, between (at least) two parties, that cannot be equitably resolved for lack of a rule of judgment applicable to both arguments" (Lyotard, *Differend*, xi). The nature of the conflict changes when it becomes clear that the people involved are speaking through different discourses, discourses that, outside of the conflict would be understood as incommensurable. Without translation, without rules that could bring these differences into alignment, the conflicts become differends. The concern of course, is that when rules *are* applied, those rules come from only one side, thus subjugating one discourse to one understood at the moment of that law's application as empowered under rule of law. It should be the goal of the law, and of the social more generally, then, to learn how to become more attenuated to this kind of conflict. Jean-François Lyotard, *The Postmodern Condition: A Report on Knowledge* (Minneapolis: University of Minnesota Press, 1984).
10. Gordon, 19.
11. Gordon, 25.
12. This is why, earlier, Lyotard had in *The Postmodern Condition* asserted that justice can learn from art, for art has the power to "allude to something which does not allow itself to be made present" (Lyotard, *Postmodern*, 80). Accordingly, "it is our business not to supply reality but to invent allusions to the conceivable which cannot be presented" (Lyotard, *Postmodern*, 80). Through the work of the imaginative, we invent possibilities by drawing relationships of figuration between the known and the unseen, and thus make visible what is occluded in a given discourse. In such presentation of the unpresentable, then, a differend might be reduced.
13. Wright, introduction to *Black Metropolis*, xx.
14. Of course, Chicago was not built on "empty," uninhabited land, though Wright's elision of a Native American presence might be read as part and parcel of his sense of the monumentality of the relationship between whites and blacks in America, a narrowness of perspective that Wright would eventually overcome. (Also see n. 8, above.)
15. Cayton and Drake have noted the extent to which "formal and informal social controls" were used to keep blacks in the Black Belt (Drake and Cayton, 175). Informal social controls included outright terrorization, for instance beatings or house bombings, while formal controls usually came in the form of restrictive covenants, which became popular in the years following the 1919 riot (Drake and Cayton, 79). Because they were often kept secret, these covenants were difficult to identify, but a 1928 edition of the *Hyde Park Herald*—the local newspaper for what was, until the 1960s, one of several exclusively white neighborhoods surrounded by the Black Belt—describes an instance when "one community member proceeded to explain the fine network of contracts that like a marvelous, delicately woven chain of armor is being raised from the northern gates of Hyde Park at 35th Street and Drexel Boulevard to Woodlawn, Park Manor, South Shore, Windsor Park, and all the far flung white communities of the South Side. And of what does this armor consist? *It consists of a contract which the owner of the property*

signs not to exchange with, sell to, or lease to any member of a race not Caucasian." (quoted in Cayton and Drake, 79)

Despite the sensational nature of physical violence, the violence enacted through restrictive covenants was a sinister violence, deadly despite their silence. It is this kind of white struggle against black mobility that Lorraine Hansberry illustrates in her classic *A Raisin in the Sun*, which is also set in Chicago. In Hansberry's play, there is relatively little display of outright violence against the Younger family, but we nonetheless witness the pernicious decay wrought by enforced segregation. In the passage above, the citizen's deep satisfaction above with the "delicate" armor is quite evident. In 1928, there were no physical gates on Hyde Park's northern border; there never have been. But as a metonym for segregation's fortifications, the "gate" is nevertheless a spot-on description of the success of these covenants, which quickly gained popularity as a way of quietly preventing the infiltration of "a race not Caucasian," namely African Americans. This is not at all to suggest that more physically violent methods were less common or less damaging. In 1923, for instance, Charles S. Johnson noted that over sixty bombs had been exploded in Hyde Park over the previous two years alone (Johnson, 113). Charles S. Johnson, "Illinois: Mecca of the Migrant Mob," in *These "Colored" United States: African American Essays from the 1920s*, eds. Tom Lutz and Susanna Ashton (New Brunswick, N.J.: Rutgers University Press, 1996). Even though he focuses on Los Angeles, Mike Davis' study, *City of Quartz*, offers several excellent accounts of how such covenants function, particularly as the weapon of choice for "Homeowner Associations" and "Citizen Councils." Mike Davis, *City of Quartz: Excavating the Future in Los Angeles* (New York: Verso, 1990). Also, Lorraine Hansberry, *A Raisin in the Sun* (New York: Vintage, 2004 [1958]).

16. Cayton and Drake, 17.
17. Victor Burgin, *In/Different Spaces: Place and Memory in Visual Culture* (Berkeley: University of California Press, 1996), 130.
18. Burgin, 133.
19. Jacques Lacan, *Écrits: A Selection* (New York: W.W. Norton, 1977), 217.
20. A psychoanalytic perspective is salient here. In "Mourning and Manic-Depressive States," for instance, Melanie Klein offers a theory regarding the process by which our experiences in the material world come to be reproduced in—indeed constitute—our unconscious worlds. She locates this capacity for "doubling" in the child's early relationship to his or her mother. She notes that through the earliest processes of incorporation, "an inner world is being built up in the child's unconscious mind, corresponding to his actual experiences and the impression he gains from people and the external world, and yet altered by his own fantasies and impulses" (Klein, 148). The thing itself becomes secondary to its representation: the experience, as the originary object, is therefore distanced from its image as it exists in the psyche. As *all* experiences are incorporated by the subject, they come to populate a psychic topos that mirrors reality. However, these images must also be improved. She adds that once "external situations which [the child] lives through become internalized—and I hold that they do, from the earliest days onwards—they follow the same pattern: they also become 'doubles' of real situations, and are again altered for the same reasons" (Klein, 149).

Once the external is brought "inside," it is subject to the same processes which dissociate internal idealized "pictures" from their referents (Klein, 148–9). It may be useful to conceptualize these doubles explicitly as versions, as tropes, as turns. Through incorporation, the subject's internal world is being "built up" and because it is subjectively altered, or rather, made continuous with the ideal self, this internal world is ultimately "inaccessible to the child's accurate observation and judgment." Moreover, this fact of interiority makes for the "phantastic nature of the inner world," and it is also for this reason the child must re-turn to the visible world for verification, as "The ensuing doubts, uncertainties and anxieties act as a continuous incentive to the young child to observe and make sure about the external object-world, from which this inner world springs, and by these means understand the internal one better" (Klein, 149). One could argue, however, that inasmuch as this necessary process of idealization hinges on the successful movement of the object from outside to inside—from the material world to the psychic—this same process potentially undermines the veracity of the visible world's "proof." Melanie Klein, "Mourning and Manic-Depressive States," in *The Selected Melanie Klein*. ed. Juliet Mitchell (New York: The Free Press, 1987).

21. Richard Wright, *Native Son* (New York: Harper Perennial, 1998), 129.
22. Culbertson, 177.
23. Wright, 19.
24. Houston A. Baker, "Giving Bigger a Voice: The Politics of Narrative in *Native Son*," in *New Essays on* Native Son, ed. Kenneth Kinnamon (New York: Cambridge University Press, 1990), 86.
25. Wright, 20.
26. Wright, 21–22.
27. Wright, 97.
28. Wright, 86.
29. Wright, 100.
30. Wright, 429.
31. Ann Petry, "Like a Winding Sheet," in *The Norton Anthology of African American Literature*, eds. Henry Louis Gates and Nellie Y. McKay, second edition (New York: W.W. Norton, 2004), 1480.
32. Petry, 1479–82, passim.
33. James Albert Ukawsaw Gronniosaw, *A Narrative of the Most Remarkable Particulars in the Life of James Albert Ukawsaw Gronniosaw, an African Prince, as Related by Himself* (North Carolina: University of North Carolina at Chapel Hill and Academic Affairs Library, 2001), http://docsouth.unc.edu/neh/gronniosaw/gronnios.html
34. Petry, 1482.
35. Wright, 405.

NOTES TO CODA

1. Black Star, "Astronomy (8th Light)," *Mos Def and Talib Kweli Are Black Star* (Rawkus Records, 2002).
2. James Baldwin, "Every Good-Bye Ain't Gone," in *Collected Essays*, ed. Toni Morrison (New York: Library of America, 1998), 775.
3. Clyde Haberman, "A Shooting, and Shooting from the Hip," Column in *New York Times*, 2/12/1999, sec. B: 1.
4. Karla F. C. Holloway, *Passed On: African American Mourning Stories: A Memorial* (Durham: Duke University Press, 2002), 6.
5. Because of how she structures *Passed On*, we know that Holloway has a sense of how and of what kinds of events this iconography has been constituted, for instance the lynching of Emmett Till. But it is important that Holloway nonetheless characterizes being impacted by such encounters as a matter of "cultural sensibility," rather than of "collective memory." By doing

so, she not only avoids having to make specific quantitative claims about the transmission of specific texts, but her choice also highlights the mundanity of such transmission.

6. Helen Epstein, "Ghetto Miasma: Enough to Make You Sick?" in *New York Times* 10/12/2003, sec. Magazine: 75–78, passim.
7. I discuss this line from Kaufman's poem, "I Have Folded My Sorrows," in chapter 5 of this book, and also the idea of the phantom limb in chapter 5. Also see chapter 1, for a discussion of what is at stake in such acts of remembering and forgetting.
8. Holloway, 6.
9. Toni Morrison, *Beloved: A Novel* (New York: Penguin, 1998), 275.
10. James Van Der Zee, *The Harlem Book of the Dead* (New York: Morgan & Morgan, 1978), 84.
11. Toni Morrison, "Foreword," in *The Harlem Book of the Dead.*
12. Jean Toomer, "Carma," in *Cane*, ed. Darwin T. Turner (New York: W.W. Norton, 1988), 12.
13. *Daughters of the Dust*, DVD, directed by Julie Dash [1991] (New York: Kino International, 2000).

Selected Bibliography

Abraham, Nicholas, Maria Torok, and Nicholas T. Rand. *The Shell and the Kernel: Renewals of Psychoanalysis*. Chicago: University of Chicago Press, 1994.
Anderson, Amanda, and Joseph Valente. *Disciplinarity at the Fin De Siècle*. Princeton, N.J.: Princeton University Press, 2002.
Andrews, William L., and Nellie Y. McKay. *Toni Morrison's Beloved: A Casebook*. New York: Oxford University Press, 1999.
Appiah, Anthony, and Henry Louis Gates, eds. *Langston Hughes: Critical Perspectives Past and Present*. New York: Amistad Press, 1993.
Baker, Houston A. "Giving Bigger a Voice: The Politics of Narrative in *Native Son*." *New Essays On Native Son*. ed. Kenneth Kinnamon. New York: Cambridge University Press, 1990. 85–117.
Baldwin, James. *Another Country*. New York: Vintage Books, 1993.
———. "Sonny's Blues" *Going to Meet the Man: Stories*. Vintage Books, 1995.
———. *Collected Essays*. Toni Morrison, ed. New York: Library of America, 1998.
———. *The Price of the Ticket: Collected Nonfiction, 1948–1985*. New York, N.Y.: St. Martin's Press, 1985.
Balfour, Lawrie. "A Most Disagreeable Mirror: Race Consciousness as Double Consciousness." *Political Theory* 26.3 (1998): 346–369.
Benjamin, Walter. "On Language as Such and on the Language of Man." *Reflections*. New York: Schocken Books, 1977.
Bergson, Henri. *Matter and Memory*. New York: Zone Books, 1988.
Bethel, Elizabeth Rauh. *The Roots of African-American Identity: Memory and History in Antebellum Free Communities*. New York: Palgrave Macmillan, 1999.
Bhabha, Homi K. "DissemiNation: Time, Narrative, and the Margins of the Modern Nation." *The Location of Culture*. New York: Routledge, 1994.
Bogumil, Mary L., and Michael R. Molino. "Pretext, Context, Subtext: Textual Power in the Writing of Langston Hughes, Richard Wright, and Martin Luther King, Jr." *College English* 52.7 (1990): 800–11.
Brogan, Kathleen. *Cultural Haunting: Ghosts and Ethnicity in Recent American Literature*. Charlottesville: University Press of Virginia, 1998.
Burgin, Victor. *In/Different Spaces: Place and Memory in Visual Culture*. Berkeley: University of California Press, 1996.
Buse, Peter, and Andrew Stott. *Ghosts: Deconstruction, Psychoanalysis, History*. New York: St. Martin's Press, 1999.
Butler, Judith. *The Psychic Life of Power*. Palo Alto: Stanford University Press, 1997.
Butler, Octavia E. *Kindred*. Boston: Beacon Press, 1988.

Castronovo, Russ. *Fathering the Nation: American Genealogies of Slavery and Freedom*. Berkeley: University of California Press, 1995.

Cheng, Anne Anlin. *The Melancholy of Race: Psychoanalysis, Assimilation, and Hidden Grief*. New York: Oxford University Press, 2001.

Chinitz, David. "Literacy and Authenticity: The Blues Poems of Langston Hughes." *Callaloo* 19.1 (1996): 177–92.

Collier, E. W. "The Phrase Unbearably Repeated." *James Baldwin: A Critical Evaluation*. T. B. O'Daniel, ed. Washington, D.C.: Howard University Press, 1977.

Crenshaw, Kimberlé. "Mapping the Margins: Intersectionality, Identity Politics, and Violence Against Women of Color." 43 *Stanford Law Review*: 1241 (1993).

Crossley, Robert. "Introduction." *Kindred*. Boston: Beacon, 1988.

Cugoano, Quobna Ottoba. "Thoughts and Sentiments On the Evil and Wicked Traffic of the Slavery and Commerce of the Human Species." *Black Atlantic Writers of the Eighteenth Century*. Adam Potkay and Sandra Burr, eds. New York: St. Martin's Press, 1995.

Culbertson, Roberta. "Embodied Memory, Transcendence, and Telling: Recounting Trauma, Re-Establishing the Self." *New Literary History* 26.1 (1995): 169–95.

Dash, Julie. *Daughters of the Dust*. Kino Video, New York, NY, 1991.

Davis, Angela. *Blues Legacies and Black Feminism: Gertrude "Ma" Rainey, Bessie Smith, and Billie Holiday*. New York: Vintage, 1999.

Davis, Mike. *City of Quartz: Excavating the Future in Los Angeles*. New York: Vintage Books, 1992.

De Man, Paul. *Blindness and Insight: Essays in the Rhetoric of Contemporary Criticism*. Minneapolis: University of Minnesota Press, 1983.

Deleuze, Gilles. *Bergsonism*. New York: Zone Books, 1988.

Derrida, Jacques. *Archive Fever: A Freudian Impression*. Chicago: University of Chicago Press, 1996.

———. *Specters of Marx: The State of the Debt, the Work of Mourning, and the New International*. New York: Routledge, 1994.

Dixon, Melvin. "The Black Writer's Use of Memory." *History and Memory in African-American Culture*. eds. Robert O'Meally and Geneviève Fabre. New York: Oxford University Press, 1994.

———. "I'll Be Somewhere Listening for My Name." *Callaloo* 23.1 (2000 [1992]): 80–3.

———. *Ride Out the Wilderness: Geography and Identity in Afro-American Literature*. Chicago: University of Illinois Press, 1987.

Drake, St Clair, and Horace R. Cayton. *Black Metropolis: A Study of Negro Life in a Northern City*. Chicago: University of Chicago Press, 1993.

Du Bois, W.E.B. *The Souls of Black Folk*. New York: Knopf, 1993.

Early, Gerald, ed. *My Soul's High Song: The Collected Writings of Countee Cullen*. New York: Doubleday, 1991.

Edmunds, Susan. "The Race Question and the 'Question of the Home': Revisiting the Lynching Plot in Jean Toomer's *Cane*," in *American Literature*, 75.1 (March 2003), 142.

Ellison, Ralph. *Shadow and Act*. New York: Vintage International, 1995.

Eng, David L. and David Kazanjian. *Loss: The Politics of Mourning*. Berkeley, CA: University of California Press, 2002.

Epstein, Helen. "Ghetto Miasma: Enough to Make You Sick?" *New York Times* 10/12/2003 2003, sec. Magazine: 75.

Equiano, Olaudah. "The Interesting Narrative of the Life of Olaudah Equiano." *Black Atlantic Writers of the Eighteenth Century*. Adam Potkay and Sandra Burr, eds. New York: St. Martin's Press, 1995.

Evans, David. "Bessie Smith's 'Back-Water Blues': The Story Behind the Song," *Popular Music* (2006), 26: 97–116.
Ford, Karen Jackson. *Split-Gut Song: Jean Toomer and the Poetics of Modernity*. Tuscaloosa, AL: University of Alabama Press, 2005.
Foster, Frances Smith. *Witnessing Slavery: The Development of Ante-Bellum Slave Narratives*. Westport, Conn.: Greenwood Press, 1979.
Foucault, Michel. *Language, Counter-Memory, Practice: Selected Essays and Interviews*. Ithaca, N.Y.: Cornell University Press, 1977.
———. "Of Other Spaces." *Diacritics* 16 (Spring 1986): 22–7.
Freud, Sigmund. *Civilization and Its Discontents*. New York,: W.W. Norton, 1962.
———. "Mourning and Melancholia." *Essential Papers on Object Loss*. Ed. Rita Frankiel. New York: New York University Press, 1917. 38–51.
———. "The Uncanny." *Collected Papers*. ed. Joan Rivere. Vol. 4. New York: Basic Books, 1959.
———. "A Note Upon the Mystic Reading Pad." Freud, Sigmund, et al. *The Standard Edition of the Complete Psychological Works of Sigmund Freud*. London: Hogarth Press and the Institute of Psycho-analysis, 1981.
———. "Remembering, Repeating and Working Through." Freud, Sigmund, et al. *The Standard Edition of the Complete Psychological Works of Sigmund Freud*. London: Hogarth Press and the Institute of Psycho-analysis, 1981. 147–56.
———. "Screen Memories." *Collected Papers*. ed. Joan Rivere. Vol. 5. New York: Basic Books, 1959.
———. "Inhibitions, Symptoms, and Anxiety: Addendum C: Anxiety, Pain, and Mourning." *Essential Papers on Object Loss*. Ed. Rita Frankiel. New York: New York University Press, 1926. 59–62.
Gates, Henry Louis, ed. *Black Literature and Literary Theory*. New York: Routledge, 1990.
———. *Figures in Black: Words, Signs, and the "Racial" Self*. New York: Oxford University Press, 1987.
Gilroy, Paul. *The Black Atlantic: Modernity and Double Consciousness*. Cambridge: Harvard University Press, 1993.
Gilyard, Keith. "Genopsycholinguisticide and the Language Theme in African-American Fiction." *College English* 52.7 (1990): 776–86.
Glissant, Édouard. "The Known, The Uncertain." Trans. J. Michael Dash. *Caribbean Discourse: Selected Essays*. Charlottesville: University Press of Virginia, 1989.
Gordon, Avery F. *Ghostly Matters: Haunting and the Sociological Imagination*. Minneapolis: University of Minnesota Press, 1997.
Gottfried, Amy S. *Historical Nightmares and Imaginative Violence in American Women's Writings*. Westport, Conn.: Greenwood Press, 1998.
Grayson, Sandra M. *Symbolizing the Past: Reading* Sankofa, Daughters of the Dust, *&* Eve's Bayou *as Histories*. Lanham, MD: University Press of America, 2000.
Griffin, Farah Jasmine. *"Who Set You Flowin'?": The African-American Migration Narrative*. New York: Oxford University Press, 1995.
Gronniosaw, James Albert Ukawsaw. *A Narrative of the Most Remarkable Particulars in the Life of James Albert Ukawsaw Gronniosaw, an African Prince, as Related by Himself: Electronic Edition*. Available: http://docsouth.unc.edu/neh/gronniosaw/gronnios.html.
Gussow, Adam. *Seems Like Murder Here: Southern Violence and the Blues Tradition*. Chicago: University of Chicago Press, 2002.
Hall, Stuart. "Minimal Selves," *Black British Cultural Studies: A Reader*. Houston A. Baker, Jr., Manthia Diawara, and Ruth H. Lindeborg, eds. Chicago: University of Chicago Press, 1996.

Halbwachs, Maurice. *On Collective Memory*. Lewis A. Coser, trans. Chicago: University of Chicago Press, 1992.

Hartman, Geoffrey H. *Holocaust Remembrance: The Shapes of Memory*. Cambridge, Mass.: Blackwell, 1994.

Hartman, Saidiya V. *Scenes of Subjection: Terror, Slavery, and Self-Making in Nineteenth-Century America*. New York: Oxford University Press, 1997.

Harvey, David. *Consciousness and the Urban Experience: Studies in the History and Theory of Capitalist Urbanization*. Baltimore: John Hopkins University Press, 1985.

———. "The Experience of Space and Time." *The Condition of Postmodernity: An Enquiry into the Origins of Cultural Change*. Cambridge, Mass: Blackwell, 1989.

———. *Justice, Nature and the Geography of Difference*. Cambridge: Blackwell Publishers, 1996.

———. *Social Justice and the City*. Baltimore: Johns Hopkins University Press, 1973.

Harvey, Lee. *Myths of the Chicago School of Sociology*. Brookfield: Gower, 1987.

Hoffman, Peter M., Cook County (Ill.). Coroner. *The Race Riots: Biennial Report 1918–1919*. Available: http://www.chipublib.org/004chicago/disasters/text/coroner/17.html

Hogan, Linda. *The Woman Who Watches Over the World: A Native Memoir*. New York: W.W. Norton, 2001.

Holloway, Karla F. C. *Passed On: African American Mourning Stories: A Memorial*. Durham: Duke University Press, 2002.

Johnson, Helene. "Poem." *This Waiting for Love: Helene Johnson, Poet of the Harlem Renaissance*, ed. Verner D. Mitchell. Amherst, MA: University of Massachusetts Press, 2006.

Hughes, Langston. *The Big Sea*. 2 vols. New York: Thunder's Mouth Press, 1986.

———. "The Collected Poems of Langston Hughes." ed. Arnold Rampersad. New York: Vintage Books, 1994.

———. *I Wonder as I Wander: An Autobiographical Journey*. New York: Thunder's Mouth Press, 1986.

Hurston, Zora Neale. *Their Eyes Were Watching God*. New York: Perennial Classics, 1998.

Huyssen, Andreas. *Twilight Memories: Marking Time in a Culture of Amnesia*. New York: Routledge, 1995.

Jacobs, Harriet. *Incidents in the Life of A Slave Girl. The Classic Slave Narratives*. ed. Henry Louis Gates. New York: New American Library, 1987.

Jarraway, David R. "Montage of An Otherness Deferred: Dreaming Subjectivity in Langston Hughes." *American Literature* 68.4 (1996).

Johnson, Charles S. "Illinois: Mecca of the Migrant Mob." *These "Colored" United States: African American Essays from the 1920s*. eds. Tom Lutz and Susanna Ashton. New Brunswick, N.J.: Rutgers University Press, 1996.

Johnson, Barbara. "Apostrophe, Animation, and Abortion," in *Diacritics*, 16.1 (Spring, 1986), 28–47.

Jones, Gayl. *Corregidora*. Boston: Beacon Press, 1986.

Kaufman, Bob. *Solitudes Crowded with Loneliness*. New York: New Directions Publishing Corporation, 1965.

Klein, Melanie. "Mourning and Manic-Depressive States." *The Selected Melanie Klein*. ed. Juliet Mitchell. New York: The Free Press, 1987.

———. "The Psychogenesis of Manic-Depressive States." *The Selected Melanie Klein*. ed. Juliet Mitchell. New York: The Free Press, 1987.

Kogawa, Joy. *Obasan*. New York: Anchor Books, 1994.

Kristeva, Julia. *Desire in Language: A Semiotic Approach to Literature and Art.* New York: Columbia University Press, 1980.

———. *Revolution in Poetic Language.* Trans. Margaret Waller. New York: Columbia University Press, 1984.

Lacan, Jacques. *Écrits: A Selection.* New York: W.W. Norton, 1977.

LaCapra, Dominick. *Writing History, Writing Trauma.* Baltimore, MD.: Johns Hopkins University Press, 2001.

Laub, Dori. *Testimony: Crises of Witnessing in Literature, Psychoanalysis, and History.* New York: Routledge, 1992.

Lefebvre, Henri. *The Production of Space.* Trans. Donald Nicholson-Smith. Massachusetts: Malden, 1990.

Long, Lisa. "A Relative Pain: The Rape of History in Octavia Butler's *Kindred* and Phyllis Alesia Perry's *Stigmata.*" *College English* 64.4 (2002): 459–83.

Lyotard, Jean François. *The Differend: Phrases in Dispute.* Minneapolis: University of Minnesota Press, 1988.

———. *The Postmodern Condition: A Report on Knowledge.* Minneapolis: University of Minnesota Press, 1984.

———. *Heidegger and "The Jews."* Minneapolis: University of Minnesota Press, 1990.

Mackey, Nathaniel. *Discrepant Engagement: Dissonance, Cross-Culturality, and Experimental Writing.* New York: Cambridge University Press, 1993.

Mercer, Kobena, and James Van Der Zee. *James Vanderzee.* New York: Phaidon, 2003.

Metress, Christopher, ed., "Afterword," *The Lynching of Emmett Till: A Documentary Narrative.* University of Virginia Press, 2002.

Morrison, Toni. *Beloved: A Novel.* New York: Penguin, 1998.

———. *Playing in the Dark.* Cambridge: Harvard University Press, 1992.

———. "The Site of Memory." *Inventing the Truth: The Art and Craft of Memoir.* William Zinsser, ed. Boston: Houghton Mifflin, 1987.

———. *Song of Solomon.* New York: Alfred A. Knopf, 1994.

———. *Jazz.* New York: Plume, 1993.

Mullen, Edward J., ed. *Critical Essays On Langston Hughes.* Boston: G.K. Hall & Co., 1986.

Murray, Albert. *Stomping the Blues.* New York: Da Capo, 1989 [1987].

Nelson, Cary. *Repression and Recovery: Modern American Poetry and the Politics of Cultural Memory.* Madison: University of Wisconsin Press, 1989.

Nielsen, Aldon L. *Writing Between the Lines: Race and Intertextuality.* Athens, GA: University of Georgia Press, 1994.

Nietzsche, Friedrich Wilhelm. *On the Advantage and Disadvantage of History for Life.* Indianapolis: Hackett Pub. Co., 1980.

———. "Why I Write Such Good Books." *On the Genealogy of Morals & Ecce Homo.* ed. Walter Arnold Kaufmann. New York: Vintage Books, 1967.

Nora, Pierre. "Between Memory and History: *Les Lieux De Mémoire.*" *Representations.* Spring. (1989): 7–25.

———. "Between Memory and History: *Les Lieux De Mémoire.*" Trans. Lawrence D. Kritzman. *Realms of Memory: Rethinking the French Past.* New York: Columbia University Press, 1996.

Notorious B. I. G. *Ready to Die.* 1 sound disc. Bad Boy Records manufactured & marketed by Universal Records, New York, N.Y., 1994.

Novick, Peter. *That Noble Dream: The "Objectivity Question" and the American Historical Profession.* Cambridge: Cambridge University Press, 1988.

O'Brien, Ellen, and Lyle Benedict. "1919: Race Riots." *Deaths, Disturbances, Disasters And Disorders In Chicago: A Selective Bibliography of Materials from the Municipal Reference Collection of the Chicago Public Library.* 2001

[1996]. Available: http://www.chipublib.org/004chicago/disasters/riots_race.html

Oliver, Paul. *Conversation with the Blues.* New York: Cambridge University Press, 1997.

O'Meally, Robert, and Geneviève Fabre, eds. "Introduction." *History and Memory in African-American Culture.* eds. New York: Oxford University Press, 1994.

O'Meally, Robert. "Checking Our Balances: Ellison on Armstrong's Humor." *boundary 2* 30:2 (2003).

Oshinsky, David M. *Worse Than Slavery: Parchman Farm and the Ordeal of Jim Crow Justice.* New York: Free Press, 1996.

Peckham, Joel. "Jean Toomer's *Cane*: Self as Montage and the Drive Toward Integration." *American Literature* 72.2 (2000): 275–90.

Petry, Ann. "Like a Winding Sheet." *The Norton Anthology of African American Literature.* Henry Louis Gates and Nellie Y. McKay, eds. 2nd ed. New York: W.W. Norton, 2004.

Proust, Marcel. *Swann's Way.* New York: Vintage Books, 1989.

Ramazani, Jahan. *Poetry of Mourning: The Modern Elegy from Hardy to Heaney.* Chicago: University of Chicago Press, 1994.

Rampersad, Arnold. *The Life of Langston Hughes.* 2 Vols. New York: Oxford University Press, 1986.

Rowell, Charles H. "An Interview with Octavia E. Butler." *Callaloo* 20.1 (1997): 47–66.

Rushdy, Ashraf H. A. *Neo-Slave Narratives: Studies in the Social Logic of A Literary Form.* New York: Oxford University Press, 1999.

———. *Remembering Generations: Race and Family in Contemporary African American Fiction.* Chapel Hill: University of North Carolina Press, 2001.

Scruggs, Charles. "Jean Toomer and Kenneth Burke and the Persistence of the Past" in *American Literary History* 13.1 (2001).

Shaffer, Marguerite S. "Selling the Past/Co-Opting History: Colonial Williamsburg as Republican Disneyland." *American Quarterly* 50.4 (1998): 875–84.

Silverman, Kaja. *Threshold of the Visible World.* New York: Routledge, 1995.

Singh, Amrijit. "Introduction." *Memory, Narrative and Identity.* Amrijit Singh, Joseph Skerrett, eds. Boston: Northeastern University Press, 1994.

Spear, Allan H. *Black Chicago: The Making of a Negro Ghetto.* Chicago: University of Chicago Press, 1967.

Spillers, Hortense J. "Mama's Baby, Papa's Maybe: An American Grammar Book." *The Women and Language Debate.* Camille Roman, et al. New Brunswick: Rutgers University Press, 1994.

Stevens, Maurice. *Troubling Beginnings: Trans(per)forming African American History and Identity.* New York: Routledge, 2003.

Tanner, Laura E. *Intimate Violence: Reading Rape and Torture in Twentieth-Century Fiction.* Bloomington: Indiana University Press, 1994.

Toomer, Jean. *Cane.* ed. Darwin T. Turner. New York: W.W. Norton, 1988.

Turner, Darwin T. "Introduction [to the 1975 Edition of *Cane*]." *Cane.* ed. Darwin T. Turner. New York: Norton, 1988.

Tuttle, William M. *Race Riot: Chicago in the Red Summer of 1919.* Urbana: University of Illinois Press, 1996.

Van Der Zee, James, Owen Dodson, and Camille Billops. *The Harlem Book of the Dead.* Dobbs Ferry, N.Y.: Morgan & Morgan, 1978.

Vidler, Anthony. *The Architectural Uncanny: Essays in the Modern Unhomely.* Cambridge: MIT Press, 1996.

White, Deborah Gray. *Ar'n't I a Woman?: Female Slaves in the Plantation South.* New York: W. W. Norton, 1999.

White, Hayden V. *The Content of the Form: Narrative Discourse and Historical Representation.* Baltimore: Johns Hopkins University Press, 1987.
———. *Figural Realism: Studies in the Mimesis Effect.* Baltimore, MD.: Johns Hopkins University Press, 1999.
———. *Metahistory: The Historical Imagination in Nineteenth-Century Europe.* Baltimore: Johns Hopkins University Press, 1975.
Woods, Gregory. "Gay Re-Readings of the Harlem Renaissance Poets." *Journal of Homosexuality* 26.2–3 (1993): 127–42.
Wordsworth, William. "Essays Upon Epitaphs." *Selected Prose Works of William Wordsworth.* Murphy. London, 1810.
Wright, Richard. *The Color Curtain: A Report On the Bandung Conference.* Jackson: University Press of Mississippi, 1995.
———. "How Bigger Was Born." *Native Son.* New York: HarperPerennial, 1998.
———. *Native Son.* New York: HarperPerennial, 1998.
Wright, Richard, Edwin Rosskam, and United States Farm Security Administration. *Twelve Million Black Voices.* New York: Thunder's Mouth Press, 1988.
Yates, Frances. *The Art of Memory.* Chicago: University of Chicago Press,1966.
Yocum, Demetrio. "Some Troubled Homecomings." *The Postcolonial Question.* eds. Iain Chambers and Lidia Curti. New York: Routledge, 1996.
Young, James Edward. *The Art of Memory: Holocaust Memorials in History.* New York: Prestel, 1994.

Index

A
Adorno, Theodor, 107
"All of Me" (Holiday), 31, 42, 50
Another Country, 30–42, 46–49, 50–51, 57–58. *See also* Baldwin, James
Armstrong, Louis, 39
"Astronomy (8th Light)," 106, 114
axé (ashé, axe), 52–54

B
backwater, 44–46, 104
"Backwater Blues," 43–46, 48. *See also* Smith, Bessie
Baker, Houston, 97
Baldwin, James, 29, 92; *Another Country*, 30–42, 46–49, 50–51, 57–58; "Discovery of What It Means To Be An American, The," 28; "Every Good-Bye Ain't Gone," 6, 106; *Fire Next Time, The*, 9; on *Native Son*, 89–90; "Sonny's Blues," ix
Balfour, Lawrie, 90
"Becky," 32n8. *See also* Toomer, Jean
Beloved: character, 111; novel, 7–9, 30, 53n11, 60, 74–5, 111. *See also* Morrison, Toni
Bergson, Henri, 29n5, 53n12, 83–84
Billops, Camille, 111
Black Chicago (Spear), 11–12
black female bodies, 51–53, 98, 104
Black Metropolis (Cayton and Drake), 90–91, 93, 94
blues, 36, 59, 63–64; as performance, 42–43, 45–46. *See also* Smith, Bessie
Bone, Thugs-n-Harmony, 108
Burgin, Victor, 95
Butler, Octavia, 76–78; *Kindred*, 75–88, 89

C
C.B. and Axe Gang, 55–57
Cane. *See* Toomer, Jean
"Carma," 52–59. *See also* Toomer, Jean
Cayton, Horace, 90–91, 93, 94
Chicago: Black Belt, the, 90, 94, 96, 99; Chicago Riots (1919), 11, 94; Great Chicago Fire, The, 94; segregation, 11, 89, 94–96, 99
Chicago School of Sociology, The, 90
collage (montage), 52n7, 112
collard greens, 10
collective memory, 29n3, 29n5, 30, 108n5
Colonial Williamsburg, 72–73, 85
Color Curtain, The, 92n8, 105. *See also* Wright, Richard
conjuring, 1, 9–10, 29–30, 34, 78, 102–103, 108
"Cotton Song," 50–51. *See also* Toomer, Jean
Crossley, Robert, 78, 79
Cugoano, Quobna Ottoba, 15–16
Culbertson, Roberta, 82–84, 86–87, 97
Cullen, Countee, 21–25, 43, 54, 63
cultural sensibility, 6, 12, 30, 60, 107–110

D
"Danse Africaine" (Hughes), 25
Dash, Julie, 114
Daughters of the Dust (Dash), 114
Davis, Angela, 43–44, 53n11
de Man, Paul, 24, 42
Derrida, Jacques, 1
Des Pres, Terrence, 83, 97

Diallo, Amadou, 106
differend, 92, 93n12
Dixon, Melvin, 13–14, 21–23, 46, 83
Drake, St. Clair, 90–91, 93, 94
Du Bois, W.E.B., 60

E

Early, Gerald, 23
Edmunds, Susan, 69n18
empathy, 5, 29, 32–34
"Empty Bed Blues," 36, 41. *See also* Smith, Bessie
Epstein, Helen, 109–110
Equiano, Olaudah, 15–16
Essence Awards, The, 108–109
"Every Good-Bye Ain't Gone," 6, 106. *See also* Baldwin, James

F

Fire Next Time, The, 9. *See also* Baldwin, James
flooding: material, 43–45; as metaphoric, 23–25, 44
Ford, Karen Jackson, 51n4
"Future Expectations" (Van Der Zee), 3, 112–114

G

ghetto miasma, 109–110
ghosts and ghostliness, ix, 1–2, 4, 8–9, 32, 52–53, 55, 64–65; "Becky," 32n8; Beloved (character), 111; figured in *Native Son*, 99–100; ghetto miasmas, 109–110; ghosting, 86. *See also* phantom
Gilyard, Keith, 76
Glissant, Édouard, 13, 14
Gordon, Avery, ix, 89, 92,
Great Chicago Fire, The, 94
Great Flood, The (1927), 45
Great Migration, The, 14, 54
Griffin, Farah, 91,
Gronniosaw, Ukasaw, 103
Gussow, Adam, 42

H

Haberman, Clyde, 106–107
Halbwachs, Maurice, 29n5
Hansberry, Lorraine, 94n15
Harlem Book of the Dead, The, 111–112
Hartman, Saidiya, 5
haunting: as interpretive practice, 5–7; as political choice, 109; difference from memory, 2; managed through aesthetic distance and experience, 43, 48, 53n11; through contemplation, 53, 60. *See also* possession; phantoms
"Heritage" (Cullen), 21–25, 43, 54, 63
Hogan, Linda, 72, 83
Holiday, Billie, 31, 42, 50
Holloway, Karla, 14, 107–109, 110, 111
"How Bigger Was Born," 93. *See also* Wright, Richard
Hughes, Langston, 16–17, 20; "Danse Africaine," 25; "Negro Speaks of Rivers, The," 16–21
Hurricane Katrina, 10. *See also* flooding (material); backwater
Hyde Park Herald, The, 94n15

I

identification, 7, 32; and empathy, 5, 32–33; and race, 6, 15, 20, 28; as reading practice, 73–74; false empathy, 6n4; in reading, 73; primordial (Nora), 29; unchecked, 5; with perpetrators, 74, 75n4
"I Have Folded My Sorrows" (Kaufman), 62–65, 110
Incidents in the Life of a Slave Girl (Jacobs), 75n4, 79
insight (*also* epiphany), 17, 46, 54, 58, 66, 70, 73, 98, 103–104
interracial relationships, 50, 86

J

Jacobs, Harriet, 75n4, 79
"Jailhouse Blues," 36, 47, 50–51. *See also* Smith, Bessie
Johnson, Barbara, 68
Johnson, Charles S., 94n15
Johnson, Helene, 25–27, 28–29
Johnson, Raynard, 9–10

K

"Karintha," 52. *See also* Toomer, Jean
Kaufman, Bob, 62–65, 110
Kindred (Butler), 75–88, 89
Klein, Melanie, 96n20
knowingness, 36, 65, 114. *See also* cultural sensibility; empathy; insight
Kogawa, Joy, 72, 73
Kristeva, Julia, 19, 25, 53n12

L
La Capra, Dominick, 5
Laub, Dori, 6
Lefebvre, Henri, 94–96
lieux de mémoire, les (Nora), 10–11, 19, 21–22, 29, 59
"Like a Winding Sheet" (Petry), 100–104
Lomax, Alan, 55–57
Long, Lisa, 74
lynching: in *Another Country*, 42; in *Cane*, 71; Johnson, Raynard, 9; Till, Emmett, 9
Lyotard, Jean-François, 92, 93n12

M
Mackey, Nathaniel, 3, 52, 64, 83
madeleine, the (Proust), 29, 61, 65
memory: difference from haunting, 2. *See also* phantoms; cultural sensibility; rememory
Metress, Christopher, 10
Middle Passage, 14, 17n12, 18–20, 23–25, 59
migrant labor, 55–58
migration, 14, 16, 20, 22, 54, 90, 93
milieux de mémoire, les (Nora), 29–30, 35–36, 54, 65, 72
Morrison, Toni: Beloved (character), 111; *Beloved* (novel), 7–9, 30, 60, 74–5; flooding (metaphor), 23–25, 44; *Song of Solomon*, 33–34. *See also* rememory
Mos Def and Talib Kweli are Blackstar, 106, 114
Mr. T, 3
"Murder Was the Case," 108–109
Murray, Albert, 42, 45
music, ix, 36, 43. *See also* blues

N
Native Son, 11, 89–93, 96–100, 104–105. *See also* Wright, Richard
"Negro Speaks of Rivers, The," 16–21. *See also* Hughes, Langston
neo-slave narratives, 78
Nietzsche, Friedrich Wilhelm, 29n4
nigger, 1, 28, 40, 52, 90, 101–103
Nora, Pierre, 10–11, 29–30, 65
nostalgia, 16n10, 29n3. *See also* sexuality
Notorious B.I.G., 4

O
Obasan (Kogawa), 72, 73
O'Meally, Robert G., 39

P
Peckham, Joel, 52n7
Petry, Ann, 11, 100–104
phantom: limbs, 83, 110; pain, 71, 72, 83. *See also* ghosts and ghostliness
photographs: "Future Expectations," 112–114; *Harlem Book of the Dead, The*, 111–112; in *Beloved*, 111
"Poem" (Johnson), 25–27, 28–29
possession, 110; and haunting, 40, 100; empathic, 6n4; racism as, 40, 103, 110; social as form of, 31–32. *See also* rememory
Proust, Marcel, 29, 60–62, 64–65, 83

R
race. *See* cultural sensibility; segregation; identification
racism. *See* ghetto miasma; segregation
Raisin in the Sun, A (Hansberry), 94n15
rap, 4
Razaf, Andy, 39, 41
reading: as haunting practice, 5–7; as memory in *Cane*, 52–54; as dialectical process in *Cane*, 52n7; and identification, 73–74; in *Kindred*, 78–81, 84–85, 89
Ready to Die, 4
rememory, 7–9, 30, 45, 53n11, 60; in *Kindred*, 83–84; in *Native Son*, 99. *See also* possession
rivers, 16–21; Harlem R., 41; Hudson R., 41–42; Mississippi R., 17–18, 23–24, 43–45
"Rosie," 55–57

S
sacrifice, 32, 42, 44, 51–52, 57, 63, 70, 102. *See also* suicide
St. Simon of Cyrene, 71n16
Scruggs, Charles, 70
segregation, 11, 89, 94–96, 99
sexuality: bisexuality, 46; homosexuality, 50; heterosexuality: compulsory, 46–50; nostalgic, 55–56, 58
shame, 47–48, 50, 76–78, 81, 98, 105
Smith, Bessie, 28; "Backwater Blues," 43–46, 48; "Empty Bed Blues,"

36, 41; "Jailhouse Blues," 36, 47, 50–51. *See also* blues
Snoop Dogg, 108–109
Song of Solomon (Morrison), 33–34
"Song of the Son," 65–71. *See also* Toomer, Jean
sonic register, 36, 90
"Sonny's Blues," ix. *See also* Baldwin, James
Southern Poverty Law Center, The, 9
spatiality, 29, 54, 67; heterotopic space, 31n7; segregation, 11, 89, 94–96, 99; space and trauma, 82, 98
Spear, Allen, 11–12
Spillers, Hortense, 20
suicide, 9, 30, 36
Swann's Way (Proust), 60–62, 65

T

Toomer, Jean: "Becky," 32n8; *Cane*, 51, 52n7, 71; "Carma," 52–59; "Cotton Song," 50–51; "Karintha," 52; lynching narrative in, 71; "Song of the Son," 65–71. *See also* reading
"Tha Crossroads," 108
Till, Emmett, 9–10, 108n5
trauma, 82–85, 97–98
Tupac Shakur, 108

V

Van Der Zee, James, 111–114

W

Walker, Kara, 4
"(What did I do to be so) Black and Blue?" 5, 39, 41
Williams, Eugene, 11–12
witnessing, 3, 5–6, 11, 18, 109
Wordsworth, William, 62
Wright, Richard: *Color Curtain, The*, 92n8, 105; "How Bigger Was Born," 93; *Native Son*, 11, 89–93, 96–100, 104–105

About the Author

Marisa Parham is Assistant Professor of English at Amherst College, specializing in literary and cultural theory and teaching classes on the poetics of African-American experience, modern American popular culture, and Anglophone literatures after colonialism. Her essays have appeared in *Callaloo* and *ELH*, and she is also the author of *The African-American Student's Guide to College.*